PASTOR CHARLES H. SPURGEON.

Spurgeon's Gold

New Selections from the Works

of

C. H. Spurgeon
Pastor of the Metropolitan Tabernacle, London, England

Selected by

Edmond Hez Swem
Pastor Second Baptist Church, Washington, D. C.

Soli Deo Gloria Publications
...for instruction in righteousness...

Soli Deo Gloria Publications
P.O. Box 451, Morgan, PA 15064
(412) 221-1901/FAX 221-1902

*

Spurgeon's Gold was first published in 1888 in Washington, D.C. This Soli Deo Gloria reprint is 1996.

*

ISBN 1-57358-039-2

*

The publisher wishes to thank the Speer Library at Princeton Theological Seminary for making this book available for publication.

PREFACE.

Spurgeon's Gold contains more than 2,400 selections—many of them the best of proverbs—from the works of Charles H. Spurgeon, the greatest of London preachers, whose sermons and books are read all over the world.

Having visited London twice and been frequently charmed by his marvelous voice and benefitted by his wonderful words of wisdom, I desire that his best thoughts may be read and remembered by those who cannot hear him and have not the leisure to search the voluminous works of the prince of speakers, great author, philanthropist, and educator.

I can never forget the petition of the prayer Pastor Spurgeon offered for me in the auditorium of the Metropolitan Tabernacle, London (the night before re-embarking for home), after I had spoken to his people and sung a solo: "May he bring thousands of souls to the feet of the Saviour and keep them there."

Dear Reader, pray that the Lord may make me a winner of many souls, and that this book may be helpful to both saints and sinners.

So oft' you heard
Of Him who lived and died and lives again,
Now trust* in Him who saves believing men,
'Though oft' they've erred.

Edmond Hez Swem.

Washington, D. C.

---

* Read John III: 16.

INDEX.

SPURGEON'S GOLD.

Right principles are spiritual gold, and he that hath them, and is ruled by them, is the man who truly lives.

The Lord would not have spirituality divorced from common sense.

Man is all outside to God.

I always delight in a man who can afford to go about his life-work without fuss, bluster, or loud announcement.

Usefulness is as possible in obscurity as in publicity.

To wait is much wiser than, when you cannot hear the fog-horn and have no pilot, to steam on and wreck your vessel on the rocks.

It is hell to live without a Saviour.

Lose your head and you lose the battle. Lose your heart and you have lost all.

In the struggle of life a cheerful fearlessness is a grand assistance.

Though you have a clear head and can stand in a dangerous place, I would not recommend you to go there if somebody else would thus be placed in danger.

Skillful mariners sail by all winds, and we ought to make progress through all circumstances.

I saw the other day the emblem of a serpent with its tail in its mouth, and if I carry it a little beyond the artist's intention the symbol may set forth appetite swallowing up itself.

Giving to God is no loss; it is putting your substance into the best bank.

Let us not seek to alter our destiny, but let us try to make the best of our circumstances.

While apostolic men looked for the coming of Christ, they looked for it with no idea of dread, but, on the contrary, with the utmost joy.

A notable divine once gave this direction: "The way to heaven is, turn to the right and keep straight on." I would add, turn when you come to the cross. Only one turn is needed, but that must be a thorough turn and one in which you persevere.

God loves to discover even the shadow of faith in his unbelieving creatures.

Sinners may go unpunished for many a bright hour of the morning of life, but as the day grows older the shadows fall and their way is clouded over.

I believe that there is not a moral truth in the Book of Proverbs which does not also wear a spiritual aspect.

The poorest way is better than none, and the humblest office is better than being out of employment.

A very small graveyard will be big enough to bury all the good people who die through giving up their drop of beer.

To go willfully into temptation is comparable to the crime of arson, in which a man collects combustible materials and secretly kindles them, that his house may be burned down.

History certainly repeats itself within the Chuch of God as well as outside of it.

Modern thought labors to get away from what is obviously the meaning of the Holy Spirit, that sin was lifted from the guilty and laid upon the innocent.

Our Lord's spirituality is not of that visionary sort which despises the feeding of hungry bodies. Look after His poor and needy ones. How can you be truly spiritual if you do not so?

He who holds back a soul from Jesus is the servant of Satan, and is doing the most diabolical of all the devil's work.

It is shameful and beyond endurance to see how genteel swindling is winked at by many.

The power to receive is scarcely a power, and yet it is the only power needed for salvation. Come along and take what Christ doth freely give you.

Suppose an accident should take away our lives; I smile as I think that the worst thing that could happen would be the best thing that could happen. If we should die, we should but the sooner be "forever with the Lord."

The publican's prayer so pleased the Lord Jesus Christ, who heard it, that He condescended to become a portrait painter, and took a sketch of the petitioner.

Pain and depression of spirit, endured in early life, have prepared many to sympathize with the unhappy, and to live a life of benevolence.

I will die with my face toward God and holiness.

If you are not saved it is not because God will not or cannot save you; it is because you refuse to accept His mercy in Christ.

Your non-searching of the Scriptures, your weariness under Gospel preaching, your want of care to understand the mind of God, is *prima facie* evidence that there is some enmity in your heart against the Most High.

If we live near to God we cannot sin without incurring sharp rebukes.

There is no having influence over the great men or the little men of this age except by being firm in your principles and decided in what you do. If you yield an inch you are beaten; but if you will not yield—no, not the splitting of a hair—they will respect you.

Would to God that the best that could happen to all men did happen to them.

The most careful driver one day upset the cart.

We are soon coming out of the eggshell of time, and when we break loose into eternity and see the vastness of the divine purposes, we shall be altogether amazed at the service bestowed, which will be the reward of service done.

Dogs will go mad with their muzzles on, and so will men sin despite the restraints of law.

Get a holy subject and keep to it till you have drawn somewhat from it to feed your soul upon, and then you will do your life-work with less fatigue, because you will have more strength to spend upon it.

Since evil thoughts are the first of sins, we had better meet the charge with immediate repentance and an instant faith in the only Saviour.

A do-nothing professor is a merely nominal member, and a nominal member is a real hindrance. He neither contributes, nor prays, nor works, nor agonizes for souls, nor takes any part in Christian service, and yet he partakes in all the privileges of the Church. Is this fair?

Salvation is a diamond with many facets.

If I begin to describe our hope, I must begin with what, I think, is always the topmast stone of it—the hope of the second advent of our Lord and Saviour Jesus Christ; for we believe that when He shall appear we shall also appear with Him in glory.

When you and I get fearful how foolishly we think and speak and act.

Our little ones are real beauties, always a pound or two plumper than others of their age, and yet it don't tire you half so much to nurse them as it does other people's babies.

It is a very rare thing to hear even the infidel rail at the character of Jesus.

If you are very busy, think and pray all the more, or your work will wear and weary you, and drag you away from God. For your work's sake, break away from it, and give the soul a breathing time.

Believe in the Lord Jesus Christ, and believe intensely.

The god of this world is the devil, and he claims implicit obedience. Sin in some form or other is the image which Satan sets up and requires us to serve.

Language is thought to be forcible because it is hard, severe, and blustering, and yet there is little power in such speaking except to provoke opposition and furnish motives and weapons for the opposer.

To use an ecclesiastical term, we stand between two Epiphanies; the first is the manifestation of the Son of God in human flesh in dishonor and weakness; the second is the manifestation of the same Son of God in all His power and glory.

Not even in this world does sin pay its servants good wages.

If the way to God and salvation is, indeed, blocked up, it is only blocked up by your own sins. The door is not locked by a divine dercee, nor nailed up by any necessity of circumstances, nor barred by any peculiarity of your case. No, there is neither block, nor bar, nor lock, except your sin.

You cannot in grace, any more than in anything else, do a great deal at once, and do it effectually.

Faults are always thick where love is thin.

Give me a man who deliberately makes up his mind, calmly sets to work, and patiently bears all rebuffs, and I know that what he sets himself to do will be done.

Accept His rule, and He will except thy prayer.

The service of God is a remunerative service; He gives wages in the work, and an abundant reward, according to His grace, when the work is done.

As voyagers cross the Atlantic, and so pass from shore to shore, so do we speed over the waves of this ever-changing world to the glory-land of the bright appearing of our Lord and Saviour Jesus Christ.

We will measure our age from our second rather than our first birth.

Baptism and the Lord's Supper will never be slighted by those whose hearts are fully possessed with love to Jesus. They may seem trifles, but if the Lord Jesus commands them they cannot be neglected.

Some soldiers are good at a rush, but they cannot form a square and stand fast hour after hour.

Jesus loves each one of His people with that same love wherewith He loves the whole of His people.

The following verses were written by Mr. Spurgeon at the age of eighteen:

IMMANUEL.

When once I mourned a load of sin;
When conscience felt a wound within;
When all my works were thrown away;
When on my knees I knelt to pray,
  Then, blissful hour, remembered well—
  I learned thy love, Immanuel.

When storms of sórrow toss my soul;
When waves of care around me roll;
When comforts sink, when joys shall flee;
When hopeless griefs shall gape for me,
  One word the tempest's rage shall swell—
  That word thy name, Immanuel.

When for the truth I suffer shame;
When foes pour scandal on my name;
When cruel taunts and jeers abound;
When "Bulls of Bashan" gird me round,
  Secure within thy tower I'll dwell—
  That tower thy grace, Immanuel.

When hell enraged lifts up her roar;
When Satan stops my path before;
When fiends rejoice and wait my end;
When legion'd hosts their arrows send,
  Fear not, my soul, but hurl at hell
  Thy battle-cry, Immanuel.

When down the hill of life I go;
When o'er my feet death's waters flow;
When in the deep'ning flood I sink;
When friends stand weeping on the brink,
  I'll mingle with my last farewell
  Thy lovely name, Immanuel.

When tears are banished from mine eye;
When fairer worlds than these are nigh;
When heaven shall fill my ravished sight;
When I shall bathe in sweet delight,
  One joy all joys shall far excel—
  To see thy face, Immanuel.

We ought to mind our thoughts, for if they turn to be our enemies they will be too many for us, and will drag us down to ruin.

You will never get to Heaven, any of you, by *playing at religion.* !!

The world has come to call an unchaste woman "unfortunate," and this is but one open expression of what it secretly believes as to all sin; it reckons our transgression to be our misfortune rather than our fault.

Unless our profession is a lie we love each other, and we must therefore show that love by our prayers for one another.

When two Christians met together who were sitting under a very lean and starving ministry, one of them comforted his fellow concerning the miserable discourse by saying: "Never mind, my friend, there is not much in the sermon, but the text is a feast by itself."

Oh, yes, beloved, if we have faith we have hope.

Though thy thirst be like that of a panting ox upon a sultry summer's day, who putteth down his mouth to the brook and drinks as though he would leave it dry, thou mayest come, and feel no trembling as to the sufficiency of the living waters.

There are certain sheep-tracks up the slopes of Scripture which are much more trodden than the rest of the holy fields.

Godliness and love can make a man, like a bird in a hedge, sing among thorns and briers, and set others a-singing too.

There is between real Christians a brotherhood which they will neither disown, nor dissemble, nor forget.

Any simpleton might be set to sniff out offensive odors; but it would require a scientific man to bring to us all the fragrant essences and rare perfumes which lie hid in field and garden. Oh, to learn the science of Christian charity!

This Bible is a letter from Him, and we prize it beyond the finest gold.

Hope as much as ever a man can hope; for when your hope is in God you cannot hope too much.

Let us seek grace to become importunate pleaders of a sort that cannot be denied, since their faith overcomes heaven by prayer.

Confession with the mouth is a sort of breaking away from the world. When a man says with his mouth, "I believe in the Lord Jesus Christ," it is as good as saying to the world, "I have done with you."

He is the devil's advocate who would judge the punishment of the impenitent to be a light one.

We hear men crying, "Lo here!" and "Lo there!" This wonder and that marvel are cried up. It would seem that the age of miracles has returned to certain hot-heads. Take ye no heed of all this. False prophets will be left in the lurch, but the word of the Lord will stand.

To keep debt, dirt, and the devil out of my cottage has been my greatest wish ever since I set up housekeeping.

It is the quiet man, the meek man, who is always hard to be turned aside from his purpose.

Some trades and callings are like a tropical climate, and their blackening effect is soon visible; certain companies are still more so; they make their mark upon the best of men, and that mark is not to their improvement.

Repent of sin and fly from it earnestly and with your whole heart.

Though we die in one sense, yet in another we shall not die, but live. We shall come forth from the land of the enemy in fullness of joy.

Standing in one of the halls of the Orphanage is *the very pulpit* from which I savingly heard the Gospel of our Lord Jesus Christ. Though I have no reverence for relics of any sort, yet a flood of grateful memories flows before me as I look upon the platform whereon stood the unknown brother who pointed me to Jesus.

He loves us better than we love ourselves.

If there were anything yet to be revealed which would render your hope a delusion at the end, you should have been made acquainted with it; Jesus Himself would break the sad news to you; He would not leave you to be horrified by finding it out for yourselves.

Don't throw away dirty water till you have got clean.

The men of this generation are even more greedy of gain, more in haste after their ambitions, than those that preceded them. They are fickle, exacting, hungering after excitement and sensation.

We are told that the teaching of God's ministers must be conformed to the spirit of the age. We shall have nothing to do with such treason to truth.

Men can with a few hasty words set loose a torrent of anger and uncharitableness, and cause the sweeping away of much good service and sweet fellowship, but who shall rule, restrain, or call back the raging flood.

The heart of the Gospel is redemption.

Sham sinners may be content with a sham Saviour; but our Lord Jesus is the real Saviour, who did really die, and died for real sin.

I believe that every flower in a garden, which is tended by a wise gardener, could tell of some particular care that the gardener takes of it. He does for the dahlia what he does not for the sunflower; somewhat is wanted by the rose that is not required by the lily; and the geranium calls for an attention which is not given to the honey-suckle. Each flower wins from the gardener a special culture.

The sorrow is sucked out of the sorrow by the lips of acquiescence.

The only matter upon which we need consolation is that poor body, which once we loved so well, but which now we must leave in the cold clay.

I have done my best to avoid dullness, and to aim at edification.

After all, we get very few cuts of the whip, considering what bad cattle we are; and when we do smart a little, it is soon over.

Prayer is good, the habit of prayer is better, but the spirit of prayer is the best of all.

All that is revealed concerning God is to me abundantly satisfactory; if I do not comprehend its full meaning, I bow before its mystery.

Every prudent merchant reckons upon a certain amount of bad debt and loss in his trading, and when it comes he writes it off as a part of his estimated charges, and is not broken-hearted.

It is all nonsense to regard religion as a selfish spiritual trade by which we save our own souls.

We can none of us tell if we go down to hell how many we shall draw with us, for we are bound to thousands by invisible bands. Over the tomb of each sinner may be read this epitaph: "This man perished not alone in his iniquity."

Doubts are all driven away when you see how believers die.

The process of spiritual quickening is not a matter of hours, but of a single second of time. I grant you, life would be very feeble at first; still, there must be a time in which it was not there at all; and, again, there must have been an instant in which it began.

I believe in sanctified afflictions, but not in sanctifying afflictions.

You will find debt to be a great dismal swamp, a huge mud-hole, a dirty ditch; happy is the man who gets out of it after once tumbling in, but happiest of all is he who has been by God's goodness kept out of the mire altogether.

Do not hope because you think yourselves pure, but come to Jesus because you are impure and need to be cleansed by Him.

It is a clear proof of the love of human nature to do evil that, when restrained from actual sin, men will rehearse their former exploits, and dote on the lusts which they indulged in years ago.

Frequently it is foolish for us poor mortals to say, "I will," because our will is so feeble and fickle.

If there were no poverty in London, it would be quite enough to break one's heart to think that there is sin in it reigning over the ungodly.

By no means put yourself in another person's power.

We do not wear our best liveries, nor say enough of the joy of being in the Lord's service, nor speak enough of the wages which our Lord will pay at the end of the day.

It is ever the singular glory of our Lord Jesus Christ that He continues to entreat, even when we continue to resist.

The open confession of our faith has a good influence upon others. How could there be a Christian church at all if every Christian man concealed his faith in his own bosom? If you love your Lord and have faith and hope in Him, do not delay to come forward and own his name and cause.

Certain scriptural doctrines are, forsooth, discarded as dogmas of the mediæval period; others are denounced as gloomy because they cannot be called untrue.

It is not everybody that will remember to keep his gunpowder out of the way of the candle.

We are refreshed by the companionship, sympathy, and advice of a like-minded comrade.

What we can give to His cause we regard as children do their spending money; we lay it out with eagerness and wish it were a hundred times as much.

Every self-righteous man is a selfish man. I am sure he is.

The Lord rejoices to blot out the transgressions of repenting sinners, for He delighteth in mercy.

If you can say that in no one action of your life, select what you may, was there anything blameworthy, anything that fell short, anything that could be censured, you say very much more than the best of men have ever claimed for themselves.

He will make thee strong upon thy knees and mighty in holy service if thou wilt but surrender thy will to Him.

I like to see the old man grow young when he talks of Christ; let him on that point become enthusiastic, even as in his boyhood.

Within the chosen family there are chastisements unknown to the outside world.

One sin might keep a man out of heaven; but the multitudes of our iniquities, the blackness, the aggravation, the repetition of our offenses made the case hopeless to all human power of wisdom.

Let us never contribute of our substance to the Master's cause with a grudging hand, as though a tax-gatherer were wringing from us what we conld ill afford.

We have seen those who dared not enter the devil's house linger long and lovingly around the door. The old woman in the fable, who could find no wine in the jar, yet loved to smell at it.

Thoughts are the eggs of words and actions, and within the thoughts lie compacted and condensed all the villainy of actual transgressions.

If you can say that you have served God and man without fault throughout all your days, you can say much more than I would venture to do. The Scripture also is dead against you when it says, "There is none righteous; no, not one."

The less we have of self the more room there is for His divine grace.

Many a man bears in his bones the sins of his youth. Around us are many who already wish that they had never been born, because of the condition into which their wantonness has brought them.

If all the gathered-out company were to pray together, what a sound of supplication would go up by reason of the multitude of men.

He who boasts of being perfect is perfect in folly.

We look upon those as royal who can risk their lives for their fellow-men, to win them liberty or to teach them truth.

A loose stone here, and a fallen tie there, and a rotting timber in a third place, will soon bring on a total ruin to a tenement, but the hand of diligence maintains the fabric. Thus must we watch our spiritual house, lest we fall by little and little.

You have not taken God to be your God if you cannot be content with Him alone.

I would sooner be blind, and deaf, and dumb, and lose all feeling than lose the sense of the beauty and perfection of God.

No criminal can be hanged a second time; one death is all the law requires; believers died in Christ unto sin once, and now they penally die no more. Our condemnation has spent itself upon our Gracious Representative.

Oh, that men would have wisdom enough not to undo in their old age what they have wrought in their youth!

Let a man get the light of God streaming into his soul, convincing him of sin, of righteousness, and of judgment to come and all reliance upon self in any form will seem to him to be the most hateful of crimes.

We might be, and we ought to be, such men and women that those who know us at home and in business would discover us to be the friends of Jesus.

What pins and needles tradesmen's bills must stick in a fellow's soul!

Many of us can bear testimony to-day that the word of the Lord is not word only, but power. It has done good to us.

This is the fault of many lives: they are squandered upon a dozen objects, whereas if they were economized for one they would be mighty lives—known in the present and honored in the future.

Ignorance is a wretched foundation, but sure knowledge is like a rock.

This is our time of schooling and dicispline, and we are learning to obey, which is the highest and best lesson of all.

Capacity for believing lies more in the child than in the man. We grow less rather than more capable of faith; every year finds the unregenerate mind farther away from God and makes it less capable of receiving the things of God.

God takes great delight in our crying to Him in the day of trouble, because there is sincerity in it.

That exhortation, "Let us hold fast," might well be written on the cover of every Christian's Bible. We live in such a changeful age that we need all to be exhorted to be rooted and grounded, confirmed and established, in the truth.

In the olden days there was a John Knox, whose prayers were more terrible to the adversary than whole armies, because he pleaded in faith.

There's always time enough to boast—wait a little longer.

Inasmuch as that salvation of God is a great one, it must have been intended to meet great sins.

It is well worth while to shake off natural timidity, which would make a good man to be as though he were dumb and deprive him of half of his usefulness. To pray in private is essential, but to be able to pray in public is profitable.

Many men are worn to rottenness in the service of their lusts.

He took our debts upon Him that He might pay them, minting his own heart to create the coinage.

There is no way to heaven but by holiness. We have need to insist much upon this in these days; for, together with laxity of thought and dubiousness of doctrinal teaching, there has come into vogue great looseness of morals.

Thinking is living.

Ah! if that question, "If ye love Me," needed to be raised in the sacred college of the twelve, much more must it be allowed to sift our churches and to test ourselves.

Only let the Lord give me oil enough to feed my lamp, so that I may cast a ray across the dark and treacherous sea of life, and I am well content.

Unkind and domineering husbands ought not to pretend to be Christians, for they act clean contrary to Christ's commands.

Whatsoever men may think of our Lord as a teacher, candor demands that they admire his example and award it the highest meed of honor.

The most fallacious estimates are made under the influence of corrupt desires. Like a judge that has been bribed, the understanding gives a false verdict.

As long as one Bible remains the empire of Satan is in danger.

In proportion as a man grows in grace he feels his dependence upon God, and, in a certain sense, his dependence upon God's people. He decreases in his own esteem and his brethren increase in his estimation.

In the dogmas of modern thought there is not enough mental meat to bait a mouse-trap; as to food for a soul, there is none of it; an ant would starve on such small grain. No atonement, no regeneration, no eternal love, no covenant; what is there worth thinking upon?

Worship is not acceptable if it be devoid of humility.

A truth may sometimes amaze you because of its greatness, but that does not stagger your faith; for your faith deals with mysteries, and is familiar with sublimities which it never dreams of comprehending.

It is well to recognize that sour speeches often proceed from a sad heart. It is wise to view ungenerous language as one of the symptoms of disease, and rather pity the sufferer than become irritated with the offensive speech.

Economy is half the battle of life; it is not so hard to earn money as to spend it well.

Remember that we have no more faith at any time than we have in the hour of trial.

God thinks no better of a tree for being burdened with rotten fruit, nor of a Church for being swollen in numbers by base pretenders.

I sicken as I think how man has plagued his fellow-men by his sins.

This life is a preparatory school, and in it we are preparing for the high engagements of the perfected.

Our Lord has a keen eye for all that is good. When He searches our hearts He never passes by the faintest longing, or desire, or faith, or love of any of His people. He says to each and all, "I know thy works."

Godliness, like murder, will out.

Love always desires to have its object near, and it has a faculty of bringing its object near. If you love anybody that person may be far away and yet to your thoughts he is close at hand. Love brings the beloved one so near that the thought of him acts upon its life.

The best rubrics of worship are those which are written on broken hearts.

Though sinful thoughts *rise*, they must not *reign*.

Jesus speaks of "twelve legions." I suppose He mentions the number twelve as a legion for each one of the eleven disciples and for Himself. They were only twelve, and yet the innumerable hosts of heaven would make forced marches for their rescue.

A man fresh from a revival meeting looks like a zealous Christian; but see him when he goes to market. As a face rendered red by the fire soon loses all its ruddiness, so do numbers lose all their godliness when they quit the society of the godly.

The resurrection comes in as an undoing of all that death has done.

It may be well to make laws to restrain fornication, theft, and blasphemy; but the only sure cure for all sins is the grace of God in the heart.

The master-magnet of the Gospel is not fear, but love. Penitents are drawn to Christ rather than driven. The most frequent impulse which leads men to Jesus is hope that in Him they may find salvation. Love wins the day. One hair from the head of love will draw more than the cable of fear.

Purity should be the mother of prudence.

Never be security for more than you are quite willing to lose.

Jesus has redeemed not only our souls, but our bodies. "Know ye not that your bodies are the temples of the Holy Ghost?" When the Lord shall deliver His captive people out of the land of the enemy He will not leave a bone of one of them in the adversary's power.

It is a pleasure to us to think of our children, for they are parts of ourselves. We could almost as soon cease to be as cease to remember them.

Oh, that the good Lord would make us correct in all points, lest we be propagators of sin through the influence of our faults.

Come, then, to the meetings for prayer, for there is the strength of the Church, and there are her Samson's locks.

I hate to hear a man exhibiting his old lusts as if they were scars of honor.

It is shocking to find men and women speaking fluently about religion, and yet their houses are a disgrace to Christianity.

I hate heard people say: "Just as I employ a lawyer to attend to my temporal business, and I do not bother my head any more about it, so I employ my priest or my clergyman to attend to my spiritual business, and there is an end of it." This is evil talk, and ruinous to the man who indulges in it.

Come, be not afraid to die, for you will travel a well-beaten track.

In troublous times our best communion with God will be carried on by supplication. Tell Him thy case; search out His promise, and then plead it with holy boldness. This is the best, the surest, the speediest way of relief.

The spirit of rebellion is the same, whatever be the manner of displaying it.

Do not be all sugar, or the world will suck you down; but do not be all vinegar, or the world will spit you out.

Lord, let me be among those who confess that they were once thine enemies, and have been reconciled to thee by the death of thy Son.

If we could read the secret history of dwarfed Christians we should find that they never had much humbling of heart.

"Look unto Me and be ye saved all the ends of the earth," was the voice of God to my soul.

Pope said, "The proper study of mankind is man." It is a deplorably barren subject. Say, rather, "The proper study of mankind is God."

When once we have passed through the iron gate and forded the dividing river, then we will begin to praise God in a manner more satisfactory than we can reach at present. After a nobler sort we will sing and adore.

Sympathy with others is not learned without personal suffering.

Since Jesus speaks after He has risen of the things that He said while He was with his disciples, we perceive that the river of death is not like the fabled Lethe, which caused all who drank thereof to forget their past.

Lord, save me from sins which call themselves little.

Patience is better than wisdom; an ounce of patience is worth a pound of brains.

It was not Luther's arguments, but Luther's plain teaching of justification by faith which shook the corner-stone of the Vatican.

The soul desires to leave the poor frail tenement of the body, but not that the body may be utterly destroyed; it quits it with the hope of having the house of clay rebuilt in a more glorious form.

Many roads lead to ruin, but only one to salvation.

I believe in the perseverance of the saints because I believe in the perseverance of the love of God, or else I should not believe in it.

When your dog loves you because it is dinner-time, you are not sure of him; but when somebody else tempts him with a bone and he will not leave you, though just now you struck him, then you feel that he is truly attached to you. We may learn from dogs that true affection is not dependent upon what it is just now receiving.

We know many persons who are always doing a great deal and yet do nothing—fussy people, people to the front in every movement, persons who could set the whole world right, but are not right themselves. Very eminent men are these!

Poverty on the back of bereavement is terrible.

Lord, lead me to count nothing my treasure but thyself, and then I may defy the thief.

A good appearance is a letter of recommendation, even to a plowman.

Better far to be morbidly sensitive and condemn one's self needlessly than to be hardened through the deceitfulness of sin.

Ah me, that so many who ought to be warriors are weaklings; that those who should be men of six feet high are so stunted as to be mere Tom Thumbs in grace.

God will never alter His terms to please you.

The most wonderful visit of all was when He came to tarry here, some thirty years and more, to work out our salvation.

When a man so courageous, so patient, as Jesus betakes Himself to cries and tears, we may be sure that the sorrow of His heart has passed all bounds. His soul within Him must have been bursting with grief. We know it was so by another sign, for the life-blood forgot to course in its usual channels and overflowed its banks in a sweat of blood.

The living child of God will have to swim against the stream.

Let us work in the full conviction that our absent Lord will soon be here again with a glorious diadem upon His brow.

Christ did not come to scare us from sin, but to save us from it.

Pain past is pleasure, and experience comes by it.

We do not believe in many ways to heaven, for we know that there is only one way.

I saw one stand up at the opening of this service to look around the Tabernacle, to see the multitude; and well he might, for it is a thing to do one's eyes good to behold this vast assembly. But what shall be our joy when we shall stand up in the midst of the great company of the redeemed? We shall look far and wide, and see no end of the great gathering.

You cannot go round to a back-door, and enter heaven by stealth.

It is better to mourn over imperfection that to be puffed up with the idle notion that there is no sin in you to be watched and conquered.

Yonder father does not need anything of his child, and yet when his birthday comes round, and there are whisperings over the house and little contributions that something may be given to dear father he is greatly pleased; he is more charmed with the little one's trifling gift than with the gold he wins on the Exchange.

New trials will bring new grace and prove the value of old promises.

Discouragement is the national epidemic of our Israel.

The evil of our life arises from the living evil within.

The disciples of a patient Saviour should be patient themselves.

Occasional actions and deeds done under pressure are no evidences of a man's condition one way or another.

Often have I read books which have awakened in my soul a sense of true brotherhood with their authors, although I have known them to be of a church opposed to many ot my own views. If they praise my divine Lord, if they speak of the inner life, and touch upon communion with God, and if they do this with that unction and living power which are the tokens of the Holy Spirit, then my heart cleaves to them, be they who they may.

He is a fool, writ large, who knows not God.

Can these things come together—mourning and resting? Oh, yes! you and I know how they meet in one bosom. I never am so truly happy as when a sober sadness tinges my joy.

When we get to heaven it will be, "Glory be to God for ever and ever and ever." We shall not hum even a single note to ourselves for our own glory or on account of any part of the work for which we deserved credit, but we shall ascribe the whole of our salvation to infinite love and undeserved favor, and to the unceasing faithfulness and power of our gracious covenant-keeping God.

The keeping of every word of God is indispensable.

Love makes no reckoning of odds.

Companionship in evil leads to a high pitch of sin.

Every man ought to have patience and pity for poverty.

The prosperity which some welcome as an unmixed favor may far more rightly be regarded as an intense form of test.

It is easy to learn how we all do it nowadays in our temples—*take off your hat, hold it in front of your face, and read the maker's name and address*; then sit down, and at the proper moment bend forward and cover your eyes, and, furthermore, stand up when the rest of the congregation do so. People get to do this just as if they were wound up by machinery; yet they do not pray when they are supposed to be praying, nor bow before the Lord when worship is being offered.

Those whom the Lord honors in public he chastens in private.

It is well that pain and anguish should cut the ropes which moor us to these earthly shores, that we may spread our sails for a voyage to the Better Land.

I feel right glad to meet with a zealous man nowadays, for zeal for God has become a rare quality in the land. You see plenty of zeal where politics are concerned. Fashion and art and society and literature each one evokes zeal of a certain kind; but we are not overdone with those who are zealous in the matter of religion.

The love of Jesus is dispersed, but not divided.

Let us learn from our Master to reckon upon forces invisible.

It is more important to be prepared to live aright than to be in an ecstasy at the thought of death.

A gentleman should have more in his pocket than on his back.

We are all in within gunshot of the enemy as long as we are this side of Jordan.

If I were to see a needle running across a table all by itself, I should know that under the table a magnet was at work out of sight. When I see a sinner running after Christ, I feel certain that divine love is drawing him; the cords may be invisibe, but we are quite sure that they are there.

Men set a high value on that which is difficult to procure.

Though we should use the purest ceremonies, multiply the best of good works, and add thereto the costliest of gifts, yet we should be unable to make ourselves clean before God.

Here is a man that was lately a drunkard, and God has loved him and made him sober, and he is wonderfully proud because he is sober. What folly! Have done, sir! have done! Give God the glory of your deliverance from the degrading vice, or else you are still degraded by ingratitude.

By and by you and I will have to die, *unless the Lord should suddenly come.*

If the Spirit be with us, there will come multitudinous conversions.

From a sweet fountain of thought we shall have sweet waters of talk.

If some of the members at our meeting were a little more spry with their arms and legs when they are at labor, and a little quieter with their tongues, they would say more for our religion than they now do.

Lord, let me think of Thee and Thy word all the while I am awake; and when I sleep, if I dream at all, let my imagination still tend Thy way.

The least particle of diamond is diamond, and the least grain of truth is truth, and therefore to be prized above the rarest gems.

Obscure the cross and you have obscured all spiritual teaching.

The most overpowering thought of all is that He loved us when there was nothing good in us whatever.

The King's highway is made through the wilderness. This highway has conducted many already to God. It is said to be a "highway and a way;" it is not only a highway by appointment, but it is a way by use and traffic.

Faith that is not warranted by the Word of God is not faith, but folly.

We never know what strength is till our own weakness drives us to trust omnipotence; never understand how safe our refuge is till all other refuges fail us.

He who is not godly every day is not godly any day.

Let us plow the heaviest soil with our eye on the sheaves of harvest, and learn to sing at our labor while others murmur.

Very small must be the number who have had fair weather all the way to glory. It is questionable if ever one has been so favored.

The most of us are but feather-bed soldiers. Our ways are strewn with roses compared with those who endured hardness in the olden time.

Difficulties imagined are apt to arrive.

The Gospel which suits little children is that which saves souls; the Gospel of the common people is the only Gospel.

You would think from some people's talk that religion is a very difficult thing, only to be understood by the cultured few. You must be a learned scientist or a scholarly critic before you can understand *the modern Gospel.* It is not so with the Gospel of Jesus. Oftentimes learned men miss this way altogether, while simple people perceive it and walk in it.

Let us watch that we never undo with our hands what we say with our tongues.

When we come to pleading terms with God, there is nothing that so helps us as to be able to quote the promise and plead, "Thou saidst."

The egg of mischief is smaller than that of a midge; a world of evil lurks in a drop of rebellion.

He who plays when he should work has an evil spirit to be his playmate.

Sermons which we have studied with care, delivered with travail, prayed over and wept over, are praised for such minor matters as taste, accuracy, and diction, and the truth they contain is not received.

Oh, my heart, take care that thou answer to the Lord like an echo! When he saith, "My love," do thou answer with the selfsame title.

Sin seems all the greater because it was committed against a sin-forgiving God.

If he that has brought me so far toward heaven does not help me throughout the rest of my journey, I must die even within sight of the Promised Land.

They used in the old times to catch pigeons and send them out with sweet unguents on their wings; other pigeons followed them into the dovecote, for the sake of their perfume, and so were captured. I would that every one of us had the heavenly anointing on our wings, the divine perfumes of peace and joy and rest; for then others would be fascinated to Jesus, allured to heaven.

Let us value Scripture as much as Christ did.

The presence of God does so stay the soul and quiet the heart that fear, which hath torment, is driven away.

Into the army of our Lord the deserter is received with gladness; but he must begin in the ranks, and must prove his fidelity before he is again entrusted with a commission.

The best doctors are Dr. Diet, Dr. Quiet, and Dr. Merryman.

A whole company of believers have been roused to hearty devotion by the fervor of one man.

Fellowship with God we must have, or the essential honey of love will be deficient, the bloom of joy will be wanting, the aroma of zeal and earnestness will be missed.

We make fearful failures with God's promises through not appropriating them.

Since the Lord has appeared to me, He has made me see His restraining hand where once I saw nothing but the cruel disappointment of my hopes.

In my own person I know what it is to be vexed with sore pains and yet to feel such rest of heart that I felt no desire to complain. When we rejoice in divine love we make small account of our bodily condition. If deaf, blind, or otherwise full of infirmities of the flesh, we make small reckoning of the whole when we know the joy of pardoned sin.

Those who are evermore making light of hell are probably doing it in the hope of making it easy for themselves.

We are bound to guard jealously every single word which He has given to us.

Alas! we do not always suffer fools *gladly*, though suffer them we do.

Sooner than let their tongues have a holiday, men would complain that the grass is not a nice shade of green, and say that the sky would have looked neater if it had been whitewashed.

Men throw away their souls in order to keep their coppers.

Peter brought out brass farthings of boasting and impetuous folly at times; but he also brought forth so much true gold that his Lord said, "Blessed art thou, Simon Barjona."

In the dust of self-abasement is the place for hope.

When you and I are risen from the dead we shall rise full of the spirit of service.

Charity towards others, abundantly practiced, would be the death of envy and the life of fellowship, the overthrow of self and the enthronement of grace.

A wise man has told us, as if it were an axiom, that the imputation or the non-imputation of sin is an impossibility. Be it so; we have become familiar with such things since we have beheld the cross. Things which men call absurdities have become foundation truths to us.

The arrears of neglected service are grim debts.

Find, if you can, one occasion in which Jesus inculcated doubt, or bade men dwell in uncertainty.

Of all matters, religion is the worst to play with. It may be easy to mimic it, but the price to be paid for such fooling will be terrible.

Disobedient children are unhappy children.

Alas! the Lord himself had his Judas, and to this day swords of brittle metal hang at the golden girdle of his Church.

The Lord's promise once given is never recalled.

Thy work may be washed away like the work of little children in the sand of the sea-shore, but that which God doeth endureth forever.

I have heard of a husband and wife who felt their love for each other to be so strong that they almost wished to go through the wedding ceremony again to show how content they were to bear the easy yoke of married love. Many of us could say the same. We would also be joined anew to our Lord.

When you are in argument for the truth, do not grow angry, for this would be to fight the Lord's battles with the devil's weapons.

The sermon is not long to you who feed upon the Word; but to those who sleep at the table it is intolerably tedious. The whole service is dreary to them, though to believers it is bright and happy.

The largest generosity must refuse some requests when it is a higher kindness to withhold than to bestow.

If hearers were better, sermons would be better.

Death can hide in a drop and ride in a breath of air. Our greatest dangers lie hidden in little things.

We care little for those who are orthodox Christians in creed if it is clear that they are heterodox in life. He who believes the truth should himself be true.

We do not hold truth in a true way unless it leads us to a true life.

But when God makes a promise He fulfills it, fulfills it, and fulfills it again and again and again, to the same man and to hundreds of other men.

If you can say, "My God," you will be bound to exalt Him. If He has given Himself to you so that you can say, "My Beloved is mine," you will give yourself to Him, and you will add, "and I am His." Those two sentences, like two silken covers of a book, shut in within them the full score of the music of heaven.

Many prosperous men owe their present position to the fact that they were faithful when they were in humble employments.

For brightness, give me not the sunlight, but that superior glory with which the Lord lights up the darkness of affliction.

One pampered sin will slay the soul as surely as one dose of poison will kill the body.

Wise men in this world are like trees in a hedge—there is only here and there one.

Verily, the race of fools has not yet died out. Thousands still think it profitable to gain the world and lose their own souls.

Worldly-wise men think us fanatics and fools, but we know what they are and where the folly really lies. Oh, that their eyes were opened to join with us in the joys which they ridicule.

The Lord Jesus Christ has nothing that He values as He does His own people.

While a man's first business is his body and the things of time and sense he is and must be at enmity with God.

It seemed almost a novelty in the church when it was stated, some years ago, that Mr. George Müller walked by faith in regard to temporal things. To feed children by faith in God was looked upon as a pious freak. We have come to a pretty pass, have we not, when God is not to be trusted about common things?

If you have great sin, remember that there is a great Saviour.

We have to magnify our Lord among men who would, if they could, again crucify Him.

We cannot too often use the weapon which the Spirit Himself calls His sword.

The preacher claims no priestly power, and therefore should never wear a peculiar dress.

If God bids us, we can sweeten water with salt and destroy poison with meat; yea, we may walk the waves of the sea or the flames of a furnace.

A true believer should tremble when the world commends him, but he should feel complimented when it utterly despises him.

Evil thoughts mainly blacken the man's own mind.

The world's catechism is, "What shall we eat? What shall we drink? Wherewithal shall we be clothed?"

As the young duck which has been reared in a dry place yet takes to the water as soon as it sees a pond, so do many hasten to evil at the first opportunity. How often it happens that those young persons who have been most shut out from the world have become the readiest victims of temptation when the time has come for them to quit the parental roof.

Your tribulations will yet yield you music.

Superstition and fanaticism shall not be gratified by either voice or dream, but yet the way of the righteous shall be made plain.

We must teach more by our example than by our advice, or else we shall be poor pleaders for the right.

Boldly come unto the King of kings, from whom no sincere petitioner ever was dismissed unheard.

The poorest may be neat.

We have had helpers after the flesh who have not been present when we wanted them—perhaps they have studiously kept out of the way; at any rate, just at the pinch, when we have said, "Oh, that so-and-so were here," our friend has been at the end of the earth; but it has never been so with God.

I know no greater joy than to be useful to your souls.

It is the part of a brave man, and especially of a believing man, neither to dread death nor to sigh for it; neither to fear it nor to court it.

While dying, to turn one's eyes to Another dying at your side, and trust your soul with Him, is very marvelous faith. Blessed thief, because they put thee down at the bottom, as one of the least of saints, I think that I must bid thee come up higher and take one of the uppermost seats among those who by faith have glorified the Christ of God!

It is the disciple's part to accept the teaching of his Master.

Child-like confidence in God shall march on as upon a raised causeway, and always find for itself a road.

The saint in his errors is a star under a cloud, but the sinner is darkness itself.

Grumbling is a bad trade, and yields no profit.

All that we see around us of force and might is but God in action. There is no such deity as "*Nature;*" *nature is the Lord at work.*

A Cæsar's revenue would discharge a poor man's liabilities and would scarcely suffer diminution; far more will the infinite merits of Jesus discharge my sins and remain infinitely full.

We are outlaws, and His atonement purges us out of outlawry and makes us citizens.

That your religion may be really solid metal, and not an imitation of it, or a mere gilded bauble, you must be tried.

Whenever the Saviour describes Himself by any emblem that emblem is exalted and expanded, and yet it is not able to bear all his meaning. The Lord Jesus fills out every type, figure, and character; and when the vessel is filled there is an overflow. There is more in Jesus, the Good Shepherd, than you can pack away in a shepherd. He is the good, the great, the chief Shepherd; but He is much more.

It is certain that more pleasure can be bought by money given to the poor and needy than by all the hoardings of a millionaire.

I doubt not it shall be one of our greatest delights while seeing the Lord's face to serve Him with all our perfected powers.

My soul, be thou in love with the way as well as with the end, since thy Lord is the one as well as the other.

The ugliest sight in the world is one of those thorough-bred loafers.

Self-denials, which seem hard at first, become delights in due season, so that we even wonder that we thought them denials.

We all make too much of the approval or disapproval of our fellow-men, who are, after all, only the spectators, and not the umpires, of the race.

We declare that among the most potent means in all the world is prayer.

Mark well our singing. Do we join in it with the heartiness, the solemnity, and the correctness which are due to Him who hears our psalms and hymns?

I spoke about the difficulty of keeping on. "Yes," answered my friend, "and it is harder still to keep on keeping on." So it is. There is the pinch. I know lots of fellows who are wonders at the start. What a rush they make! But then there is no stay in them; they soon lose breath.

Follow the Lord, for where the road is rough thou wilt be less likely to slip than in more smooth and slippery places.

Our Lord, after he had risen from the dead, was still full of the spirit of service, and therefore he called others out to go and preach the Gospel, and he gave them the Spirit of God to help them.

The agreement of two saints is a grand force, against which very few obstacles can stand.

It is not how much we have, but how much we enjoy, that makes happiness.

Most guilty men, when their crimes are exposed, blame their ill-luck and not their evil hearts.

Some men treat the law and testimony of the Lord as if it were like plaster of Paris, to be poured over their features to take the cast of their own boasted loveliness.

Sin is the gall of bitterness; a drop of it would turn an ocean of pleasure into wormwood.

It is difficult to realize it, that our divine and innocent Saviour placed Himself in such a condition for our sakes that His needs were manifold.

What more treacherous than one's temper? In a sudden gust of passion you utter words of anger. How gladly would you recall them! but they are registered. Down into the ditch of despondency you sink. For days to come you feel that you cannot forgive yourself.

Your adversity may prove your advantage by offering occasion and opportunity for the display of divine grace.

It is an essential part of the education of a Christian to learn the promises.

Certain minds will learn anything from those they love and nothing from those who are masterful with them.

There is wisdom in generosity.

We ought as naturally to seek after the Lord from day to day as the spark seeks the sun, or the river the ocean, or the sheep its pasture, or the bird its nest.

We have had enough to do with watching over our own hearts and endeavoring to bring sinners to Christ without becoming more nice than wise upon matters of theological subtlety and word-spinning.

Truth may not prevail to-day or to-morrow, but her ultimate victory is sure.

I have found by long experience that nothing touches the heart like the cross of Christ.

We ought to have an intense longing for the salvation of all sorts of men, and especially for those, if there are any, that treat us badly. We should never wish them ill, not for a moment; but in proportion to their malice should be our intense desire for their good.

Men make engagements thoughtlessly, and before long they realize that it would be ruinous to keep them.

I had no fault to find with him except this grave fault—that he was seldom at home, was not master of the house, and could not control his children.

If I were to choose a trade I would select one which gave me leisure for the service of the Lord Jesus.

Silence seldom makes mischief.

He who is discovered by his real excellence and not by his egotistical advertisement of his own perfections is a man worth knowing.

Satan knows that we would never consent to give up a wheel of the Gospel chariot, and therefore in his craftiness he only asks for the linch-pins to be handed over to him.

The heart of man is the seed-plot of iniquity and the nursery of transgression.

When grace is absent there is no meaning in ritual; it is as senseless as an idiot's game.

The Greek Liturgy fitly speaks of "Thine unknown sufferings;" probably to us they are *unknowable* sufferings. He was God as well as man, and the Godhead lent an omnipotent power to the manhood, so that there was compressed within His soul and endured by it an amount of anguish of which we can form no conception.

Those that fight against the Lord of Hosts are not agreed among themselves; they shall sheathe their swords in each other's bosoms.

Prayer is an ever open door.

Sinners run fearful risks when they appeal to justice; their wisdom is to cast themselves upon free grace.

If they were not fools they would not be idlers.

Never say, "Nobody will see me," for you will see yourself, and your conscience will turn king's evidence against you.

We must capture hearts for Jesus by showing that we are of like passions with them, and love them much. Love men to Jesus—that is the art of soul-winning.

God can bless our littleness and use it for His glory.

Persons of sensitive disposition and sedentary habits are prone to seek a righteousness of inward feeling.

There will be no climbing the hill of the Lord without effort; no going to glory without the violence of faith. I believe that the ascent to heaven is still as Bunyan described it—a staircase, every step of which will have to be fought for.

It is not easy to avoid injuring others.

An infinite serenity shall keep our body, soul, and spirit throughout eternity.

A sentinel must not leave his post even to gather pearls or diamonds; nor must we forsake our duty in order to acquire the highest honors.

If we never have headaches through rebuking our little children, we shall have plenty of heartaches when they grow up.

It is a mere assumption, though some state it with much confidence, that inability removes responsibility.

Wheels are tapped with a hammer on the railway that their soundness may be tested. Not only does affliction thus try our characters, but prosperity does the same.

The real cure for covetousness—namely, contentment. This is a rare drug in the market.

Unbelief calls you to go from improbability to impossibility; from extravagance to romance; from romance to raving.

Our dear babes go home because "He gathereth the lambs with His arms and carrieth them in his bosom;" and our ripe saints go home because the Beloved is come into His garden to gather lilies. These words of our Lord Jesus explain *the continual home-going;* they are the answer to the riddle which we call death.

The Lord has a faithful company that hold fast the faith and will not let it go.

Satan is always doing his utmost to stay the work of God.

A fallen one, when restored, may have gained in self-knowledge, but he must necessarily be a loser in many other respects.

All heads are not sense-boxes.

Delayed answers are not only trials of faith, but they give us an opportunity of honoring God by our steadfast confidence in Him under apparent repulses.

It is true the Church is not so full of life and energy and power and spirituality and holiness as she was in her first days, and therefore some insinuate that the Gospel is an antique and effete thing; in other words, that the Spirit of God is not so mighty as in past ages. Instead of blaming the Holy Ghost, would it not be better for us to smite upon our breasts and chasten our hearts?

If we follow not the way of distinction from the world we are not following Christ.

It shall be well for any minister if it may be written upon his tombstone, "He never preached what he did not practice." How many today, would qualify?

Know that verily you are a piece of gold, or else you would not have been put into the furnace.

Idle men tempt the devil to tempt them.

The child has to go to bed, but it does not cry if mother is going upstairs with it. It is quite dark; but what of that? The mother's eyes are lamps to the child. It is very lonely and still. Not so; the mother's arms are the child's company and her voice is its music.

The choicest communications ever made to human minds are those which have come from the Great Father.

Certain herbs yield no smell till they are trodden on, and certain characters do not reveal their excellence till they are tried.

Wealth to the worldling is not wealth to the Christian. His currency is different, his valuables are of another sort.

A church is a congregation of faithful men—that is to say, of men who are believers in the Lord Jesus, men in whom the Holy Spirit has created faith in Christ, and the new nature of which faith is the sure index. The one Church of Jesus Christ is made up of all believers throughout all time. Just as any one church is made up of faithful men, so is the one Church of Christ made up of all faithful churches in all lands, and of all faithful men in all ages.

Hold the old faith, and hold it in the old fashion, too.

God has not merely pitied us from a distance and sent us relief by way of the ladder which Jacob saw, but He hath Himself visited us.

Do you not know that a person who is silent when a wrong thing is said or done may become a participator in the sin? If you do not rebuke sin—I mean, of course, on all fit occasions, and in a proper spirit—your silence will give consent to the sin, and you will be an aider and abettor in it.

Only when you are out-and-out for Jesus can you be in a right condition.

The possession of a God or the non-possession of a God makes the greatest possible difference between man and man.

Cannon have been called "the last arguments of kings;" but the name of Jesus is the master argument of the King's children

Neither the wise nor the wealthy can help him who has long refused to help himself.

Any one sin willfully indulged and persevered in is quite sufficient to prove a man to be a traitor to his God.

The Church is not formed to be a social club, to produce society for itself; not to be a political association, to be a power in politics; nor even to be a religious confederacy, promoting its own opinions; it is a body created of the Lord to answer his own ends and purposes, and it exists for nothing else.

If there were no heaven to miss and no hell to merit, sin is a curse upon this life. How differently would some of you hear if you did but remember that in the Gospel God Himself in person comes to you!

The labor of the foolish in spinning a righteousness of their own, that is neither accredited by the divine law nor by the holy Gospel, is almost incredible; they would rather give their bodies to be burned and their goods to feed the poor than submit to salvation by grace, though it is the only possible salvation.

The difficulties of unbelief are ten times greater than the difficulties of faith.

He that speaks truly will not run back from his promise.

That religion which needs no care and takes no trouble is in great demand in the world.

Idleness is the key of beggary.

Who, then, are they that laugh at faith? Rationalists? Nay; irrational men, at war with one of nature's first and most essential laws.

Surely the good Lord means to convince the Church of her own powerlessness that she may cast herself upon the divine might. Looking around she can see no help for her in her enterprise; let her look up and watch for His coming who will bring her deliverance. Amid apparent helplessness the Church is rich in secret succors. When the time cometh for the Lord to make bare His arm, we shall see greater things than these, and then we shall wrap our faces in a veil of blushing confusion to think that we ever doubted the Most High.

The sin of doing nothing is about the biggest of all sins, for it involves most of the others.

Every day I say to myself:

> "What though my eye of faith be dim,
> I'll hold on Jesus, sink or swim."

It is written, "The blood of Jesus Christ His Son cleanseth us from all sin." I have often heard the text quoted with the "us" left out; permit me to put it in at this moment—"cleanseth *us* from all sin." Now, put yourself into the "us." Dare to believe that grace admits you there.

He is making his own damnation sure if he is robbing his creditors and yet professing to be a Christian.

I fear you have more ability than you will give an account of with joy at the last great day.

Lord, I had rather take the worst from Thee than the best from Thine enemy.

Somewhere or other in the worst flood of trouble there always is a dry spot for contentment to get its foot on, and if there were not it would learn to swim.

My soul, thou canst not know or understand all things, else wert thou omniscient, and that is the prerogative of God alone.

I am persuaded that if any Church desires to be much honored of the Lord in these days, both as to internal happiness and external usefulness, it will find that the nearest way to its desire is to be wholly consecrated to the Lord.

Live in such a way that any day would make a suitable topstone for life.

Sin is like a ladder. Few reach the height of iniquity at once; the most of men climb from one evil to another, and then to a third and a fourth.

The harlot—she strays into the house of God and feels that she has no right to be there, and yet the day comes when she stands behind the Master washing His feet with her tears and wiping them with the hairs of her head, because she has had much forgiven.

Men do not pray and supplicate unless they have greater need than this world can satisfy.

I do not find it necessary, when I talk with the bereaved, to comfort them at all concerning those that are asleep in Christ as to their souls. We know that they are forever with the Lord and are supremely blessed and therefore we need need no further comfort.

A mind stuffed with vanity and unbelief must be worse than clothes stuffed with straw.

No flies will go down your throat if you keep your mouth shut, and no evil speaking will come up.

Since the way to heaven is heavenly and the road to bliss is bliss, who will not become a pilgrim?

Our own experience leads us to the conclusion that critics of others and noisy talkers of all kinds have usually some design of their own and are working to their own hand.

We had better quit our professions if we do not live up to them!

Emblems to set Him forth may be multiplied as the drops of the morning, but the whole multitude will fail to reflect all His brightness.

It may be that we shall not die; our Lord Jesus may come before we fall asleep; but if he do not come speedily, we shall find that it is appointed unto all men once to die. We shall pass from this world unto the Father by that common road which is beaten hard by the innumerable feet of mortal men.

You have gone, perhaps, to the extreme of sin; He has gone to the extreme of atonement.

"Am I an earnest laborer together with God, or am I, after all, only *a laborious trifler*, an industrious doer of nothing, working hard to accomplish no purpose of the sort for which I ought to work, since I ought to live unto my Lord alone."

A little sin unrepented of will be as fatal as a gross transgression.

Many see more with one eye than others with two, and many have fine eyes and cannot see a jot.

Praise finds out the crack of pride, wealth reveals the flaw of selfishness, and learning discovers the leak of unbelief.

Lord, be pleased of thy great mercy to overrule the vast amount of poverty and suffering which is now in this land, that men may be driven to Thee thereby.

Make sure of your footing when you stand; make double sure of it before you shift.

It is a sin not to rejoice. I will not say it harshly; I should like to say it as softly and tenderly as it could be put.

The last new book, perhaps the last sentimental story, will win attentive reading, when the divine, mysterious, unutterable depths of heavenly knowledge are disregarded by us. Alas, my brethren, too many eat the unripe fruit of the vineyards of Satan, and the fruits of the Lord's vines they utterly despise!

Between us and heaven once lay the tremendous Alps of sin.

"Oh," you say, "if I were to begin I should not keep on." No; if *you* began perhaps you would not; but if *He* begins with you *He* will keep on.

Foul is fair to me if the Lord appoints it in love.

Laziness is in some people's bones and will show itself in their idle flesh, do what you will with them.

The developing power of tribulation is very great: faith, patience, resignation, endurance, and steadfastness are by far the best seen when put to the test by adversity, pain, and temptation.

With my Lord before me, I am a traitor to him if I chink the pieces of silver in my hand and accept a present satisfaction in barter for higher things.

Experience teaches. This is the real High School for God's children.

Wagon-loads of sermons have been lost upon you—will you now believe on Him?

You sometimes see a railway carriage or truck fastened onto what goes before, but there is also a great hook behind. What is that for? Why, to fasten something else behind, and so to lengthen the train. Any one mercy from God is linked onto all the mercy that went before it, but provision is also made for adding future blessings.

An honest heart and an honest hand must be found in every man who is to be justified at the last great day.

The learned at this hour scoff at the Book, and accuse of bibliolatry those of us who reverence the divine Word, but in this they derive no assistance from the teaching or example of Jesus.

When the devil's work seems good it is at its worst.

Many people are born crying, live complaining, and die disappointed.

A scare is not a conversion. A sinner may be frightened into hypocrisy, but he must be wooed to repentance and faith.

"I sought the Lord, and he heard me," is better argument than all the Butler's Analogies that will ever be written, good as they are in their place.

Silence is often more emphatic than speech.

I do not want to have any of you remaining in spiritual infancy; we long to see you come to the fullness of the stature of perfect men in Christ Jesus.

Your reward is not what you get at present, but it lies in the glorious future. *When the Lord Jesus comes* He will reward all His stewards and servants. No truth is more plain in the four Gospels than this fact, that when Jesus returns to this earth He will distribute recompense in proportion to work done.

A Christian's business ought to be the best done of any man's in the world.

Supposed friends have left us, even as the swallows quit in our wintry weather; but we are not alone, for the Father is with us.

We have known persons of small talent and position influence their superiors by their zeal.

All are not working men who call themselves so.

Our pastoral observation over a very large church has led us to expect to see terrible failures among those who carry their heads high among their brethren.

To rise in His resurrection, to live because he lives, to be crowned in His coronation, and to be glorified with His glory, this is a double—yea, a sevenfold bliss.

Heaven and all its joys are to be had upon believing.

Even if sin be speedily repented of, its damage is not readily repaired; if its writing be erased you can see where it used to be.

It is a wretched business for a man to call himself a Christian, and have a soul which *never peeps out from between his own ribs.* It is horrible to be living to be saved, living to get to Heaven, living to enjoy religion, and yet never to live to bless others and ease the misery of a moaning world.

Breathe the air, and the air is yours; receive Christ, and Christ is yours.

Every one in Christ, man or woman, hath some testimony to bear, some warning to give, some deed to do in the name of the holy child Jesus.

O Lord, save me from all deceit and, above all, prevent my deceiving myself.

An ounce of health is worth a sack of diamonds.

If the watcher forsakes his post it will not avail that he climbed a mountain or swam a river; he was not where he was ordered to be.

The limit which is set to prayer—namely, that if we ask anything *in accordance with God's will* he heareth us, is just such a limit as love on God's part *must* fix, and as prudence on our part must approve.

That blessed Book is *a love-letter from God*, the great Father.

The imperfections of the perfect are generally more glaring than those of ordinary believers.

It is said of the peasants around Nice that they seem to have no thought of anything but how they can make a living and save a little money, and I am afraid they are by no means a singular people; in some form or other the world is in all men's hearts and thoughts. The dust of earth has blinded eyes that were meant for heaven.

Malice is seldom specific in its charges.

There is an old proverb which says of So-and-so that he was "as sound asleep as a church." I suppose there is nothing that can sleep so soundly as a church.

Lord, bit and bridle me, I pray Thee, and never let me break loose from Thy divine control.

Let us, then, be careful that we do not hurt our neighbor in so tender a point as his character, for it is hard to get dirt off if it is once thrown on.

O Lord, thy LOGOS is my *logic;* thy *Testament* is my *argument;* thy *Word* is my *warrant.*

We see around us those who are much hindered in holy living by the fact of their being wealthy, and yet perhaps we are pining to run in their silken sack.

We are so dull and carnal that our affections are soon captured by earthly objects.

When we think of God's delight in us and His love to us, is it not shameful that we should have been so seldom engaged in devotion toward Him.

Sin is carried away into the silent land, the unknown wilderness. By nature sin is everywhere, but to believers in the sacrifice of Christ sin is nowhere. The sins of God's people have gone beyond recall. Where to? Do not ask anything about that. If they were sought for, they could not be found; they are so gone that they are blotted out.

I do implore men to give up every kind of public work till they have first done their work at home.

It is not ours to improve the Gospel, but to repeat it when we preach, and obey it when we hear.

The missionary spirit is the spirit of Christ—not only the spirit of Him that died to save, but the spirit of Him who has finished His work, and has gone into His rest. Let us cultivate that spirit, if we would be like the Jesus who has risen from the dead.

With children you must mix gentleness with firmness; they must not always have their own way, but they must not always be thwarted.

Like thy servant David, I would hate every false way.

Because we make appointments for ourselves and forget the appointments of God, we meet with many more disappointments than would otherwise fall to our lot.

If there were no hell hereafter, it would be hell enough to me not to enjoy everlasting love.

As it is idle with day-dreams to fascinate the heart into a groundless expectation, so it is equally foolish to increase the evil of them by forebodings of to-morrow.

He that rejoices in the Lord always will be a great encouragement to his fellow-Christians. He comes into the room; you like the very look of his face. It is a half holiday to look at him; and as soon as ever he speaks he drops a sweet word of encouragement for the weak and afflicted.

The spirit of the age is the spirit of proud self-sufficiency.

Many a time it has cost honest minds great grief to feel that, though they are willing enough to do what they have engaged to do, yet they have lost their ability to perform their word.

If we seek a temptation we shall soon find it; and within it, like a kernel in a nut, we shall meet with sin.

Grin and bear it is the old-fashioned advice, but sing and bear it is a great deal better.

It is a matter of fact that, by smarting for one fault, gracious men learn to avoid others.

When a sincere believer tells of his own experience of the Lord's faithfulness it has a great charm about it. We like to hear the narrative of a journey from the traveler himself.

We sometimes judge the condition of religion too leniently, or else we err on the other side, and judge too severely.

Godliness is a life-long business.

I am glad to hope that some men are converted to God amid war and earthquakes and pestilence; but I am inclined to be suspicious of that kind of conversion, for fear it should die with its cause.

Many men are fondly persuaded that either they need no saving or that they can save themselves.

If men become obedient by compulsion, but would disobey if they dared, then their hearts are not right before God, and their actions are of little worth.

My very soul boils within me when I think of the impudent arrogance of certain willful spirits from whom all reverence for revelation has departed.

Commit all your secrets to no man.

When faith is broad and large, love knows that all matters which grieve the minds of His servants touch the heart of the Master, and that all which works our good works also his delight.

Trust in the Lord and use medicine too; but of the two evils—faith in God and no use of means, or use of means and no faith in God—we should certainly prefer the former.

Sin is the great plague and pest of our lives.

Sin is a contradictory thing which blows hot and cold; it hurries men, like fitful winds, this way and that, yet never in the right direction.

When a door has to be shut to save life, there is no use in half shutting it. If a person may be killed by going through it, you had better board it up, or brick it up. I want to brick up the dangerous opening of self-confidence, for it leads to deception, disappointment, and despair.

Obedience must have love for its mother, nurse, and food. The essence of obedience lies in the hearty love which prompts the deed rather than in the deed itself.

You may even go so far as to court persecution from selfish motives.

He who found a Moses to face Pharaoh, an Elijah to face Jezebel, can find a man to confront the adversaries of to-day.

But some will say that they cannot help having bad thoughts; that may be, but the question is, Do they hate them or not?

In religion everything artificial is ridiculous, or worse; but grace in the heart is *the best "master of the ceremonies."*

He has a golden master-key which excels all others: it is the operation of His own most gracious Spirit by which entrance is effected into hearts which seemed shut up forever.

Live diligently. Live while you live.

Men work for what they can get by working and pray for that which can by no other means be obtained.

When a man is easily reminded of a thing it shows that it is agreeable to him to think of it. We are sure that God's heart is much wrapped up in the covenant of grace, since the feeble cries of His children remind Him of it.

Do not reckon to live unnoticed, for a fierce light beats about every Christian.

Christianity does not come into a nation to break up its arrangements or to break down its fabric. All that is good in human society it preserves and establishes.

Some people make a great deal of common sense, and well they may, for it is the most uncommon of all the senses.

Why, at home you are at home, and what more do you want? Nobody grudges you, whatever your appetite may be, and you don't get put into a damp bed.

Can a man command the Lord? Yes, to believing men He puts Himself at their call.

It is a pity that some men carry their heads so high above their fellows all the day, for they will have to sleep at night in the same bed of clay with those whom they despise.

Anything that hurts the home is a curse.

There must be a present conscious enjoyable pardon of sin, else there would be no joy in the world for thoughtful minds.

I always feel a suspicion of those converts who get up and glibly boast that once they were drunkards, thieves, blasphemers, and so forth. Brother, if you do tell the story of your sin, blush scarlet to think it should be true.

Oh happy man, to know no scepticism, but heroically to believe!

There are many ungodly people still in the world who are not happy in the condition in which they find themselves. The present does not content them, and they have no future from which to borrow the light of hope.

I have heard talk of "a larger hope" than the Gospel sets before us; it is a fable, with nothing in Scripture to warrant it.

To keep out vain thoughts, it is wise and prudent to have the mind stored with choice subjects for meditation.

There is something nobler in falling by the woodman's strokes than in perishing by a little worm at the root. The meanness of decaying into corruption while standing in the midst of a Church is awful.

He who is a moral monster was not always such. By sinning much he learned to sin more.

Do not wish to have your portion in this life, lest you get it; for then you will be as the ungodly.

"*Be sober.*" And does not that mean, first, moderation in all things? Do not be so excited with joy as to become childish. Do not grow intoxicated and delirious with worldly gain or honor. On the other hand, do not be too much depressed with passing troubles.

To the righteous man death is not now a penalty, but a mode of going home.

He is a very good Christian man in his own esteem, but he also knows a good glass of wine, and is most fluent when he is getting far into the bottle. Have drunkards any hope of eternal life?

It seems as if the devil had muzzled some of you, so that you dare not take the good things of the Gospel to yourselves.

From henceforth let no man trouble me with doubts and questionings ; I bear in my soul the proofs of the Spirit's truth and power, and I will have none of your artful reasonings.

If all poor men's wives knew how to cook, how far a little might go.

Sinners hate each other while they wander in their different ways ; but when the Lord brings them together by His grace, then love is born in their hearts.

What is the daffodil without its golden crown, or the crocus without its cup of sunshine? Such is man without the object of his life.

It is the rule with the truly great to think most highly of others.

When the decree of God is our delight, we feel no abhorrence to anything which he appoints, either in life or in death.

A mouse was caught in a trap, the other day, by its tail, and the poor creature went on eating the cheese. Many men are doing the same ; they know that they are guilty and they dread their punishment, but they go on nibbling at their beloved sins.

His home-going pledges Him to come and compels us to look for Him.

It is not the performance of pompous ceremonies, it is not bowing and scraping, it is not using sacred words, but it is crying to God in the hour of your trouble which is the most acceptable sacrifice your spirit can bring before the throne of God.

A boaster and a liar are first cousins.

Though cruel men may desire thine ill and devise mischief against thee, thou art safe enough until the Lord shall be pleased to let loose the lion, and even then thou shalt suffer no permanent injury.

I find in the story of the brave days of old the same confessions and the same lamentations which we utter now.

Out of a dove's nest we expect only doves to fly. The heavenly life breeds birds of paradise, such as holy thoughts, desires, and acts; and it cannot bring forth such unclean birds as lust, and envy, and malice.

God suffers no foes to trespass on the domain of Providence.

If you mean to dare the infernal terrors, I can do no less than ask you to know what you are at.

When the Holy Spirit comes into the heart He finds that we know so much already of what it were well to leave unknown; we are self-conceited, we are puffed up. We have learned lessons of worldly wisdom and carnal policy, and these we need to unlearn and deny.

Our wonderful variety of wants is met by His wonderful variety of excellences.

Make thou good use of thy God, and especially gain the fullest advantage from Him by pleading with Him in prayer.

Nothing profits a man which is done carelessly.

When a man is proud as a peacock—all strut and show—he needs converting himself before he sets up to preach to others.

It is of no use reckoning that every egg in our basket will become a chicken, for it will not so happen, and our over-anticipation will be the cause of needless sorrow to us.

It is of the nature of the Lord's people to assemble themselves together and live in companies. Wild beasts may roam the woods alone, but sheep go in flocks.

Selfishness is never worse than when it puts on the garb of religion.

He who keeps the crown of the causeway, though he may hear the lion roar, shall not meet it in the way. No ravenous beasts shall be found there, for the way is not to their mind. There is one lion which those who make Jesus their way need never be afraid of—that is the lion of unpardoned sin.

Christian people are doing to-day what their forefathers would have loathed. Multitudes of professors are but very little different from worldlings.

There is always something to hoped for in the Christian's life.

We sigh for men cultured and trained in all the knowledge of the heathen; nay, but if we sought more for unction, for divine authority, and for that power which doth hedge about the man of God, how much wiser should we be.

Sinners take more pains to go to hell than the saints to go to heaven.

I never yet saw a minister worth his salt who had not some crotchet or oddity.

When the very air seems to be laden with error and vice, believers should set a double watch as to what they hear and where they go.

Others we see who are impeded by their poverty, and yet this need not be, for some of the Lord's poor are far ahead of other runners, and keep up all the better pace because they have so little to carry.

It is sweet to live in the thoughts of those we love.

We are apt to impute to Omnipotence a crushing energy which can scarcely take account of little and feeble and suffering things.

If any of you have been brought to the Lord Jesus Christ by the ministry of any man whom God favors with his help, then that man must live forever in your hearts, and be remembered in your prayers. You cannot escape from the obligation of intercession for the man who brought you to Jesus.

We are not free from the worldliness which puts self first and God nowhere, else our various enterprises would be more abundantly supplied with the silver and the gold which are the Lord's, but which even professing Christians reserve for themselves.

The sins of our youth will give us many a twist fifty years after they have been forgiven.

Look before you leap, lest a friend's advice should do you more mischief than an enemy's slander.

Oh, be not Judas to Him who is Jesus to you!

Let us hold mutual discourse upon our experiences, make pleasant exchange of our knowledge, and aid each other by our gifts.

That profession which is merely on the surface, like the gilt upon the gingerbread at a country fair, is too poor a thing to enter heaven.

There is a singular stickiness about gold and silver.

Few go wrong when they pray over their movements *and use the judgment which God has given them.*

Instead of evil thoughts being less sinful than evil acts, it may sometimes happen that in the thought the man may be worse than in the deed. He may not be able to carry out all the mischief that lurks within his designs, and yet in forming the design he may incur all the guilt.

Sinner, thou needest not look for any good thing in thyself.

Since conversion some of us have been led in a strange way, and every step of it has shown us that the Lord is good and true and ought to be trusted without stint.

This is the spirit out of which fiends are made: first, neglect, then omission, then treachery and rebellion.

The wisest course is to keep out of the way of a man who has the complaint called the grumbles.

Let the profligate judge for himself whether he is one grain better than the greediest skinflint whom he so much ridicules.

Lord, let me be as low and unnoticed as Thou pleasest, but do enable me to bear fruit to the honor of Thy name and to the comfort of Thy people.

The cross is the center of history.

Each day has its mercy, and should render its praise. Fresh are the dews of each morning, and equally fresh are its blessings.

God is in love with you. I think Aristotle said that it was impossible for one to be assured of another's love without feeling some love in return. I am not sure about that; but I think it is quite impossible to enjoy a sense of God's love without returning it in a measure.

I believe our Lord takes infinite delight in a soul which He has new created. The Church of God depends not upon learned or moneyed men, but upon those who beseech God in supplicating faith.

For the world to come between us and our Lord is very easy, but very terrible.

Whatever falls from the skies is, sooner or later, good for the land; whatever comes to us from God is worth having, even though it be a rod.

It is well to edify saints as well as to benefit ourselves.

Does it not mean that we are in Christ as the birds are in the air, which buoys them up and enables them to fly? Are we not in Christ as the fish are in the sea? Our Lord has become our element, vital, and all surrounding. In Him we live, and move, and have our being. He is in us and we are in Him. Without Him we can *do* nothing and we *are* nothing. Thus are we emphatically in Him.

At the house of the happiest knocks the hand of death.

He who is equal with God deigns to hang upon the cross and die. I know of nothing that seems more out of rule and beyond expectation than this.

If you make an idol of a child, either that child will die or something else will happen which will make your idol to be your burden. If you want to kill your husband, idolize him. If you desire ill to a beloved one, set him up in Christ's place.

He will not call you His friend unless your are exceedingly careful to please Him in all things.

Discouragement is very natural; it is a native of the soil of manhood.

We can procure our own sorrow, but we cannot produce our own comfort.

Suffer me to be the least among Thy true children rather than the chief among pretenders.

They tell us there is as much of a tree under as above ground, and certainly it is so with a believer; his visible life would soon wither were it not for his secret life.

The sons of God, the twice-born.

I put no fine face upon it—you are not perfect, no, not one of you; for "All have sinned and come short of the glory of God."

One said to me when I was troubled, "Have you not a gracious God?" I answered, "Certainly I have." He replied, "What is the good of having Him, then, if you do not trust Him?" I was sore smitten by that reply, and felt humbled in spirit.

The hardest blow that He ever laid upon His child was inflicted by the hand of love.

If we were greater students of God, how much happier we should be.

What poor creatures men are, and yet they dare to boast!

Think much, but say little; be quick at work and slow at talk; and, above all, ask the great Lord to set a watch over your lips.

As heaven and hell will never unite, so must it be plain that a saint and sin will never come together on any terms whatever.

It is a materialistic expression, but there is something more in it than mere sentiment, that there remains among the substance of this globe a sacred relic of the Lord Jesus in the form of that blood and water. As no atom of matter ever perishes, that matter remains on earth even now. His body has gone into glory, but the blood and water are left behind. I see much more in this fact than I will now attempt to tell.

When nothing else is left you God remains and God appears.

How often does it happen that those who are rejected of men are accepted of God.

It is no slight sin to discourage holy zeal and perseverance in others. May we never be guilty of killing holy desires, even in children? How often has a burning desire in a boy's heart been quenched by his own father, who has thought him too impulsive or too ardent!

What the Spirit of God has written in this inspired Book is truth to us, and we allow no human teaching to rank side by side with it.

Unexpected help shall come to us when affairs are at their worst.

While we are ready for service, it is sweet also to be ready for glory.

I have no patience with those who throw the blame on God when it belongs to themselves.

Preoccupation of mind is a great safeguard from temptation. Fill a bushel with corn and you will keep out the chaff.

This is a cheering thought for all believers, that the Lord has set apart him that is godly for Himself. He has taken measures to *preserve* all His chosen from all those who would defile and destroy them. He sets a hedge about them in providence, so that nothing shall by any means harm them. He has shut them up from the enemy and sealed them up for perpetual preservation.

We cannot calculate the range of moral influence; it is immeasurable.

If anybody were to ask me to state the Gospel in a few words, I should answer—the Lord says, "Behold Me, behold Me."

If you look down the list of the servants of God you will find that the most of them die before the object which they had in view is fully accomplished. It is true that we are immortal till our work is done; but then we usually think that our work is something other than it is.

Nothing holds a man like his word, and nothing so fully fixes the course of action of the Lord our God as His own promise.

It is in our prosperity that we are tested. Men are not fully discovered to themselves till they are tried by fullness of success.

We do not believe in fate—a blind, hard thing.

Every girl thinks she could keep house better than her mother.

Wounds are eloquent orators with a tender-hearted surgeon; expose your wounds to Jesus, and he will bind them up.

Blunders are made about men, who should ever be esteemed according to their native worth, and not according to their position and office.

He has made you, and not you yourselves, and He that made you ought to have the use of you.

There will be a remarriage of soul and body, and we shall be perfected, even as our risen Lord. Oh, the glory of that expected end!

I am bound to mention among the curiosities of the churches, that I have known many deeply spiritual Christian people who have been afraid to rejoice. Much genuine religion has been "sicklied o'er with the pale cast of thought!" Some take such a view of religion that it is to them a sacred duty to be gloomy.

Do not kick against suffering, for in so doing you may be fighting against God.

Satan is very cunning, and knows how to change his argument and yet keep to his design.

Sin is a serpent which moralists cannot tame, charm they never so wisely.

True Christians will endeavor to make their houses temples, their meals sacraments, their garments vestments, and all their days holy days.

This age also inclines greatly to those who have cast off the restraints of God's revelation and utter the flattering inventions of their own boasted "thought." Your liberal spirits, your large-hearted men, your despisers of the old and hunters after the new—these are the idols of many.

The most difficult part of the training of young men is not to put the right thing into them, but to get the wrong thing out of them.

What a pity that there is not a tax upon words.

You must serve God with a single eye to the glory of God. If you attend a prayer-meeting, or teach a class, or preach a sermon, you must not do it with a view to your ownselves in any way, or it cannot be accepted.

Unholy living is following upon unbelieving thinking.

What have we to do with consequences? It is ours to do the right, and leave results with the Lord.

It is about the best thing that happens to a Christian man when worldlings cut his acquaintance. "Come ye out from among them," is to many a severe command; but all difficulty is removed when the world turns out from us, and casts out our name as evil.

It is absolutely certain that God will hear the prayers of His people.

Sign nothing without reading it, and make sure that it means no more than it says.

A look of vexation, or a word coldly spoken, or a little help thoughtlessly withheld, may produce long issues of regret.

Work up the conversation till it reaches a fit stage for bringing in the Lord Jesus and saving truth; but be sure that you never get men's minds ready, and then fail to do that which you are aiming at.

The most *spiritual people must eat* to live.

Willful people make up their mind, and then pray; and this is sheer hypocrisy.

Many of us now contemplate the approach of death with a calm quiet patience of hope. As our years advance we are not distressed with the thought that the time of our departure draws daily nearer.

It were worth while for the whole Church to die rather than any truth of Scripture should be given up.

Sinners would like to be uplifted beyond all fear of death, they would like to be as happy as Christian people are; but they do not want to pay the price—namely, obedience to God by faith in Jesus Christ.

Godly people roof in the mansion with their prayers.

I never did see either a perfect horse or a perfect man, and I never shall till two Sundays come together.

The devil does not keep to his own side of the road, but drives in where we least expect him.

It is always better to be openly without an attainment than to bear the form of it without in reality possessing it. A sham is a shame; an unreal virtue is an undoubted vice.

Night stretches her bat's wings, and is gone; she flies before the arrows of the advancing sun.

Sin may be exhausted, the race may be numbered, time may be finished, and need may be ended, but mercy endureth forever.

When we love some favored one we like to think of all our love passages in years gone by; and the Lord so loves His people that even when they are under His chastening hand He still delights to remember His former loving-kindnesses.

Our faith deals with what God says, not with what learned men think.

God gives none up until they fatally resolve to give themselves up, and even then His good Spirit strives within them as long as it is possible to do so, consistently with His holiness.

Hang up self-confidence on a gallows high as that whereon Haman was suspended, for it is an abominable thing.

Happy is he who is happy in his children, and happy are the children who are happy in their father.

White signifies perfection; it is not so much a color as the harmonious union and blending of all the hues, colors, and beauties of light.

Sin is the blast which withers all the flowers of life.

Abused and misrepresented both by good and bad, we learned to set small store by the judgment of men, so that when praise and flattery followed we had an antidote for the poisons.

If you plead for certain mercies definitely and distinctly, with firm, unstaggering faith, you shall richly succeed.

Those who die daily will die easily. I would to God we had learned this lesson. Let us live as dying men among dying men, and then we shall truly live. This will not make us unhappy, for surely no heir of heaven will fret because he is not doomed to live here forever.

Obedience cannot be learned at the university, unless it be at the College of Experience.

Man must come distinctly *to Him*, and not to ceremonies, or sacrements, or priests, or churches, or assemblies, or creeds, or services, or doings, or feelings. There lies thy hope, and there alone.

Oh, the depravity of our nature! Some doubt whether it is *total* depravity. It deserves a worse adjective than that.

Don't go to law unless you have nothing to lose; lawyers' houses are built on fools' heads.

There are many divisions among men into nationalities, ranks, offices, and characters; but, after all, the deep divisions will always be two—the enemies and the servants of Christ Jesus.

An unholy person will fall out with sin because it has injured his health or his credit, or has brought him into difficulties with his neighbors; but when these temporary results are ended he falls in love again with the same iniquity.

Man's pride may carry him far if he is a great fool; but let him not suffer his pride to carry him into hell, for it certainly will never carry him out again.

One brother who is quarrelsome can keep a whole church in trouble. One fellow knocking about the boat may stop the oarsmen, rend the sails, and run the boat on a rock. Oh, that the peace of God may be with *all* the saints in *all* the churches!

Sometimes there is very much in words. Vital truth may hinge upon one word.

Cheerfulness is most becoming in Christian men.

The Lord loves the cry of the broken heart, because it distinctly recognizes Himself as the living God in every need sought after in prayer. From much of outward devotion God is absent.

It is a misery of miseries that you should stand on such a vantage ground as many of you do and yet be lost.

Be shy of people who are over polite, and don't be too fast with those who are forward and rough.

I have learned, dear friends, that at the Red Sea of affliction we see most of the right arm of God.

In business men put out their money, foregoing its use themselves that it may, after a while, return to them with increase; but carnal men are all for keeping the bird in the hand, and cannot wait for joys to come.

God is never at a loss for agents.

Others may break the bread to more people, but they cannot break better bread than the Gospel which you teach, for that is bread from our Saviour's own hand.

Some, too, have hindered the children because they have been forgetful of the child's value. The soul's price does not depend upon its years.

We need not ask for more talents; we have quite as many as we shall be able to answer for.

Any fool can drink; in fact, many are great fools because they drink too much of poisonous liquors. Drinking is peculiarly the common-place act of sinners.

It is a very important thing indeed that we should begin well. The start is not everything, but it is a great deal

Long ago my experience taught me not to dispute with anybody about tastes and whims.

Happy is that man who shall reach heaven unharmed and harmless, having neither gotten nor given a wound.

We have seen a child in a field of flowers filling its little hand eagerly and then dropping its posy, not for better but for other flowers. Many professors are such children.

The world has never known a period less hopeful to the Gospel than the present.

If we would but thoroughly enjoy what God has freely given us, we should be happy to the full, and even anticipate the joys of heaven.

Let us even desire to see our names in *the celestial conscription.* Let us be willing to be dealt with just as our Lord pleases. Let no doubt intervene; let no gloom encompass us. Dying is but going home—indeed, there is no dying for the saints.

The man who will be guided by nobody is usually guided by some one more foolish or more knavish than himself.

What God is doing to us in the way of trouble and trial is but his acknowledgment of us as true heirs, and the marks of his rod shall be our proof that we are true sons.

If anybody thinks that he can change a heart by his own power, let him try with any one he pleases, and he will soon be at a nonplus.

Men are not angels, remember that; but they are not devils, and it is too bad to think them so.

The life of Jesus is a roll of cloth of gold, of the manufacture of which the art is utterly lost.

Sin is a bleeding at the heart. It is a disease which destroys the true life within, as well as the fruit of it without; therefore let every man beware of flattering himself that he is right with God because no glaring vice is manifest in his daily conversation.

Vast is the difference between the chastisement of love and the infliction of justice.

Let us not have a cupboard love for God because of His kind providence; but let us love Him and praise Him for what He is and what He has done.

The day of grace is never past to any soul that lives, as long as it is willing to believe in Jesus.

The oppression of the poor in their wages, the taking of undue advantage in trading, the incurring of debts without hope of being able to pay, and the like—these are varied forms of dishonesty, and are full of injury to others.

Ours not to ask the reason, ours not to dispute about whether the deed is essential or non-essential; ours to obey right lovingly.

If, indeed, the Lord be our refuge and strength, we are entitled to seek after a spirit which shall bear us above the dreads of common men.

This great city (London) is like a seething caldron, boiling and bubbling up with infamous iniquity.

Each page of the copy-book of life is marred with errors and blots; therefore the great Teacher pities his poor scholars.

The more spiritual the duty, the sooner the soul wearies of it. An illustration of this is seen in the case of Moses, whose hands grew weary in prayer, while we never read that Joshua's hands hung down in fight.

My will has fallen into God's will as a brook falls into a river.

I have often said that I never know which to admire most, the incarnation of the Son of God or the indwelling of the Spirit of God.

God requires not only that thou shouldst do that which is right, but that thou shouldst think that which is right, that thou shouldst love that which is right, ay, and that thou shouldst be that which is right.

✓ You and your sins must part, or God and you cannot be friends.

The soul was drifting, and it fancied that the Church and the world were no longer what they were, just as men in a boat fancy that the shore is moving.

You must come right out from the love of sin if you would be delivered from the guilt of sin.

Love when it turns to jealousy is the fiercest of all passions.

It is dreadful to think that a vile imagination, once indulged, gets the key of our minds, and can get in again very easily.

I venture to say that the bulk of Christians spend more time in reading the newspaper than they do in reading the Word of God.

It will be an awful thing to be mere empty barrels, and never know it till death deals a blow with his rod of iron and we answer to it with hollow sounds of despair.

Those who are non-workers lose much by not keeping pace with those who are running the heavenly race.

Who among us would wish to realize in his own person the fabled life of the Wandering Jew, or even of Prester John? Who desires to go up and down among the sons of men for twice a thousand years?

It is a very great sin indeed to hinder anybody from coming to Christ.

The corporeal absence of our Lord from our midst might seem to be a great loss to us; but we rejoice in it because it is for His own greater glory.

It is a very good thing for Christians to be in the church; but if you are in the church before you are in the Lord you are out of place.

Keep clear of the man who does not value his own character.

If you mourn that you are not only a sinner, but *the* sinner with the definite article, the sinner above all others, you may still hope in the mercy of the Lord.

Some texts are great candles, and have found out many; but probably there is not one tiny taper of Holy Writ which has not shed its saving beams on some one or other of the Lord's precious ones.

However great the promise, it is as sure as it is great.

It is a rule with miracles, as well miracles of the Spirit as miracles of the body, that God never does what others can do. God equips us to do certain things. When circumstances enter our lives we are incapable of handling on our own, HE steps in!

Contentment should be natural to those who are born of the Spirit of God; yea, we ought to go beyond contentment, and cry, "Blessed be the Lord, who daily loadeth us with benefits."

Every mind needs a fixed point; we must have infallibility somewhere; my infallible guide is Holy Scripture.

An aged woman once said that if the Lord Jesus Christ really did save her, He should never hear the last of it. Join with her in that resolve.

God has more regard for faith than for all else that earth can yield Him.

Beware of no man more than of yourself; we carry our worst enemies within us.

In one single moment, ay, while the clock is ticking, Jesus Christ can take the scales from a blind man's eyes and let in such a flood of daylight that he shall see heaven itself.

When self is our principle and end we rise no higher than ourselves, but when God becometh the life of our soul we follow after Him, and rise far above the highest point to which nature could conduct us.

We must always be in earnest if we would be disciples of our earnest Lord.

Pray for all ministers and workers, but pray also for me. I am of all men the most miserable if you deny me this.

I admire the wisdom of Job, that he does not shirk the subject of death, but dwells upon it as an appropriate topic, saying: "I know that Thou wilt bring me to death, and to the house appointed for all living."

You have not come before—that was wrong; but the times of your ignorance God winketh at, and bids you come *now*.

Do you claim to have been absolutely perfect before your Maker from your childhood? Surely you must have a brow of brass to make such a boast.

Scripture says, "Owe no man anything," which does not mean pay your debts, but never have any to pay.

A flaw in the foundation is pretty sure to be followed by a crack in the superstructure. Do see to it that you lay a good foundation.

We care not to be conspicuous as the poplar or majestic as the cedar, but we would be useful as the olive.

The musician will be moving his fingers upon the table as if he were playing a tune; the sailor will roll about in his walk on shore as if he were still on board ship; and even so will the soul that communes with God rehearse its joys when it is busy with other matters.

I trust not to my love of God, but to God's love to me.

God's dealings with his chosen are often so mysterious that they cannot know them till they know Himself.

I believe, dear friends, that if we are right-minded every doctrine of the Gospel will make us glad, every promise of the Gospel will make us glad, every precept of the Gospel will make us glad.

Drunkenness and idleness clothe a man with rags; these are the livery of sin.

God will not overlook thee in the day when He gathers His own. He will not forget thee, thou weakest of all the flock. Thou art needful to the completeness of the company.

Perhaps more than any other man I am faced by my own inefficiency and inability to address such an audience so often, and to print all that is spoken.

I confess it very quietly, but I have often wished that I had a little congregation, that I might watch over every soul in it; but now I am doomed to an everlasting dissatisfaction with my work, for what am I among so many?

A wise father does not care to restore a son to a position for which he has proved himself to be unfit. Even so has the Lord dealt with many backsliding ones; like David, they have been restored, but never to their former peace, prosperity, and power.

My word is of no value at all, except as it is made up of the essence of the divine Word.

If you know these two things—yourself a sinner and Christ a Saviour—you are *scholar enough to go to heaven.*

Beware of every one who swears.

Surely, the devils themselves would at the first have scarce believed it, that there could exist a race of creatures so hardened as to refuse the love which visits them in grace.

If you do not mean to serve Christ, at least stand out of the road and let other people serve Him.

We all need the truth to come home to us with personal and forcible application, for we are always inclined to shift unpleasant inquiries upon others.

Another deluge, more desolating even than the former, will come if ever the Church forgets her high calling and enters into confederacy with the world.

There's no use in lying down and doing nothing because we cannot do everything as we should like.

He who has to deal with young lambs or little children has great need to guard his movements.

Past time urges us to diligence, for it has reported us in heaven; and future time calls us to earnestness, for it must be short and may end this very day. AND THEN!

Love is both the source and the channel and the end of the divine acting.

He that serves God in body, soul, and spirit, to the utmost of his power, finds new power given to him hour by hour, for God opens to him fresh springs.

Language is a poor vehicle of expression when the soul is on fire; words are good enough things for our cool judgment, but when thoughts are full of praise they break the back of words.

A good man in a house is good store to the family. A converted daughter, a praying son, a holy husband, a gracious wife—why, these are the pillars, the ornaments, the buttresses of the house.

In any business, never wade into water where you cannot see the bottom.

Our temptation will be to think we could do exceedingly well in somebody's else sphere, but that we may be pardoned if we do not shine in our own.

While God lives, truth is in the ascendant.

In the resurrection the body shall be quickened, and the resurrection shall be to the body what regeneration has been to the soul.

We have known houses turned into stables or menageries by those whose love, which should have gone out to human beings, went out to dogs and cats. People must have objects of affection, and if they have not the better they choose the worse.

That pretty nonsense which some prattle about—"a larger hope."

In the midst of human sin, if the trumpet were sounded "up and away," you would be glad to hear it that you might speed to the fair land, where sin and sorrow will never assail you again.

Believers do not escape the sorrows of this life; but, then, no sorrow that comes to a Christian is sent as a penal infliction. It is not sent as a vindication of law, but as a tender parental discipline.

God can soon cut short our usefulness, and he will do so if we cut short our love.

Alas! a spiritually thirsty soul is a choice rarity. Where shall I find him? With what joy will I salute him! He is the man who will gladly receive the tidings of Jesus and His love.

There is no shield for a guilty soul like the blood-red shield of the atonement.

The thorn-crown commands homage as no other diadem ever did, for it braces men into heroes and martyrs No royalty is so all commanding as that which has for its insignia the chaplet of thorn, the reed, the red cloak, and the five wounds.

If sin were not so deceitful it would not be half so destructive as it is.

We have seen men who were quite fair where their hats covered their foreheads, and thoroughly bronzed where the sun had looked upon them. A man's heart had need be covered with a veil of holy carefulness, or the world will get at it and brown it with evil.

Patience has a golden hand.

It is wonderful how little a person can live on if he will but keep himself in proper check and consume only that which is absolutely needful.

By the ardor of prayer and the confidence of faith we may be caught up into Paradise, and there utter words which are beyond the latitude of earth, and are dated "from the Delectable Mountains."

Holy perseverance is a great desideratum.

You may lose a great deal *for* Christ, but you will never lose anything *by* Christ. You may lose for time, but you will gain for eternity; the loss is transient, but the gain is everlasting.

It is not necessary to happiness that a man should be prosperous in business or applauded by mankind; it is only needful that the Lord should smile on him.

Evil thoughts are the marrow of sin.

Let us go in for winning the ten pounds, if we can. For our Lord's sake let us trade in spiritual things with all our hearts.

We need more meditation, more of this shooting of thought-arrows at a mark on which they will strike and stick, more of this throwing the thought-ball at the wall that we may catch it again.

You, my dear friend, have a little faith; it is not much bigger than a grain of mustard-seed, but faith of that size has great power in it.

The hearer of the Gospel is bound to be a repeater of the Gospel. We are all called upon, as we know the Lord, to tell to others what the Lord has told to us; and if we do not so, we are guilty of disobedience to a great Gospel precept.

It were a sad sentence if we were bound over to dwell in this poor world forever.

Are we not satisfied to take our lot with the holy men and women who already sleep in Jesus.

When marriage is *merry-age* it is natural to desire a long life of it; but when it is *mar-age* the thought of parting is more endurable.

What if I call it "a superfluity of naughtiness" to doubt Him whose life and death are crowded with infallible proofs of his unchanging love to us.

Nobody is so wise but he has folly enough to stock a stall at Vanity Fair.

This is one of the things we want very much—that every member of the Church should recognize that he is ordained to service.

Among the early Christians the relatives of martyrs were a sort of aristocracy, and the martyrs themselves were regarded as the nobility of the Church. We need a spice of the same spirit at this day.

I have no desire to be famous for anything but preaching the old Gospel.

We hurry through this Vanity Fair; before us lies the Celestial City and the coming of the Lord, who is the King thereof.

Let us estimate children at their true valuation and we shall not keep them back, but we shall be eager to lead them to Jesus at once.

Example is a great fashioner of character.

If you are enabled to rise above fear in times of alarm then will those who see you say, "This is a man of God and this is God's work upon his soul.

I joyfully expect to meet many of you in heaven, and to know you, and to commune with you. I should not like to float about in the future state without a personality, in the midst of a company of undefined and unknown beings. That would be no heaven to me.

We must watch even in the safest places, lest in an hour when we are not aware we should be battered and bruised by some mighty evil.

Sins and debts are always more than we think them to be.

Men do not usually care to spend a pound in the hope of getting back a groat and no more, and yet when the soul is given up for the sake of worldly gain the loss is greater still, and not even the groat remains.

"Thou shalt not kill," may be broken by anger, hate, malice, and the desire for revenge.

If the Supreme should say, "Live here forever," it were a malediction rather than a benediction.

We must be willing to hook on anywhere; be leader or shaft-horse; be first or last; be sower or reaper, as the Lord ordains. Have no choice, and then you will find satisfaction.

It is more necessary for us that we should make a discovery of our faults than of our virtues.

The very things which men most dread, namely, the falling of mountains and the gaping open of the earth, will become the desire of terrified sinners at the last.

Do not trick yourself out in the weeds of your own repentance, much less in the fig-leaves of your own resolutions, but come to God in Christ Jesus in all the nakedness of your sin and everlasting mercy will cover both you and your sins.

When God means a creature to fly he gives it wings, and when he intends men to preach he gives them abilities.

Desire no other forces for God's work than God Himself ordains to use.

As I am sure to seek after that which I desire, and am sure to desire that which I conceive to be happiness, it is clear that my conception of happiness will largely regulate my whole course of life.

Those who are most pure and honorable have yet their shortcomings and errors to mourn over.

The way to heaven by works is only possible to a man who is absolutely perfect; and none of you are in that condition.

We do not believe in the *Kismet* of blind fate, but we believe in the predestination of infinite wisdom, and therefore we say, "It is the Lord, let him do what seemeth to him good."

When faith evaporates there is a speedy departure of spiritual power.

We are getting on in years, some of us, but we do not wish to feel old; at least, we want to keep as much of the freshness and joy of youth as we well can.

I have sometimes wished that I had nothing else to do but to dwell with God in prayer, praise, and preaching. Alas! one has to come down from the mount of the transfiguration and meet the lunatic child and the quarrelsome scribes at the bottom of the hill.

Hundreds would never have known *want* if they had not first known *waste.*

Has it ever struck you how much the life of Christ with His people lay in intense familiarity with them?

Let it not be thought that faith is contrary to reason. No; it is not unreasonable for a little child to believe its father's statements, though it be quite incapable of perceiving all their bearings.

When a sinner knows that his salvation does not lie in himself at all, but wholly in Christ, then he discovers the great secret.

Some time ago a person who wanted, I suppose, to make me feel my own insignificance, wrote to say that he had met with a number of negroes who had read my sermons with evident pleasure, and he wrote that he believed they were very suitable for what he was pleased to call "niggers." Yes, my preaching was just the sort of stuff for niggers. The gentleman did not dream what sincere pleasure he caused me, for if I am understood by poor people, by servant-girls, by children, I am sure I can be understood by others.

May God drive every unconverted sinner into a corner, and so compel him to yield to grace.

Though you mourn over the disciples, rejoice over their Master.

✓Let it never be forgotten that when a man is down he has a grand opportunity for trusting in God.

Few men can keep up a deceit when they approach their end.

In certain crafts and trades there are selfish reasons for keeping their knowledge a secret, but nothing of this kind can appertain to the profession of godliness. Having found this honey, so abundant and so free to all comers, nature itself bids us call our brethren to see our treasure and urge them to partake of its sweetness.

A bold man took this motto: "While I live I'll crow;" but our motto is: "While I live I'll praise."

It seems as if the Master might pass over sin in a thousand others, but He cannot wink at failure of love in His own espoused one.

Some persons have no hope, or only one of which they might justly be ashamed. Ask many who deny the Scriptures what is their hope for the future. "I shall die like a dog," says one. "When I'm dead there's an end of me." If I had such a wretched hope as that, I certainly would not go about the world proclaiming it. I should not think of gathering a large congregation like this and saying to you: "Brethren, rejoice with me, for we are all to die like cats and dogs." It would never strike me as a matter to be gloried in.

That man who says "It is my Father's will" is the happy man.

Men turn their faces to hell and hope to get to heaven; why don't they walk into the horse-pond and hope to be dry?

No man comes to the Father but by the Son, and no man long keeps to the Father who does not keep to his faith in the Son.

The carrion which professors can now feed upon is disgusting to the very thought of a real Christian. Entertainments are got up among religious people which are unworthy even of decent worldlings. Many true hearts are deeply wounded by this terrible degeneracy. Were it not for a small remnant we had been as Sodom, and been made like unto Gomorrah.

Lord, let me never be what I cannot be forever.

I have lived to see many brilliant projects lighted and left to die out in smoke. I have heard of schemes which were to illuminate the world, but not a spark remains.

None of us can wish our departed friends back from their thrones. Since they have gone to be where Jesus is and to enter so fully into the most blissful fellowship with Him and the Father, we would not have them return, even for an instant, to this poor country. We only wish that our turn for migration may come soon. We would not be too long divided from our fellows.

When will you cease to censure others and reserve your severity and your critical observations for your own conduct?

The art of stretching is uncommonly general nowadays. Unseen showers of frogs fall regularly when newspapers are slack.

The wealth of nations is nothing to the wealth of Jesus.

Princes should behave as princes. Their haunts should be in palaces and not amid dung-heaps. How, then, is it that some who profess and call themselves Christians are found raking in questionable amusements to discover pleasure, and many others groping amid sordid avarice to find satisfaction in wealth.

Nothing will oil the wheels of the chariot of life so well as more of the praising of God.

The introduction of a holy thought into carnal minds is a miracle as great as to get a beam of light into a blind eye or a breath of life into a dead body.

It is as great a marvel as the making of a world that any one of our race should attain to righteousness.

What can the devil offer the joyous Christian? Why, if he were to say to him: "I will give thee all the kingdoms of the world and the glory thereof if thou wilt fall down and worship me," the believer would reply to him: "Fiend, I have more than that. I have perfect contentment; I have absolute delight in God." The devil will speedily quit such a man as that, for the joy of the Lord is an armor through which he cannot send the dagger of his temptation.

Dog won't eat dog, but men will eat each other up like cannibals, and boast of it, too.

We are enriched when we lose fictitious virtues.

We have seen a hedge all thick with dry leaves throughout the winter, and neither frost nor wind has removed the withered foliage, but the spring has soon made a clearance. The new life dislodges the old, pushing it away as unsuitable to it. So our old corruptions are best removed by the growth of new graces.

The unregenerate man has always an idol. He will worship anything rather than his God; yea, he will sooner worship himself than his Saviour.

Our faith is at home in wonderland, where the Lord's thoughts are seen to be as high above our thoughts as the heavens are above the earth.

Constantly keep up your confession. There are times when you will be inclined to put your flag away into the canvas case and hide your coat-of-arms in the cellar. Then you may fitly judge that the devil is getting advantage over you, and that it is time that you ceased to be beguiled by his sorceries. Tear up the wrappings, throw the bag away, and nail your flag aloft where every eye can see it.

The age is growing more and more irreverent, unbelieving, indifferent.

Every one can see that there is a grave distinction between sins of infirmity and willful transgressions. A man may splash us very badly with the wheel of his carriage as he passes by, and we may feel vexed, but the feeling would have been very much more keen if he had thrown mud into our face with deliberate intent.

Some people were born on the first of April, and are always hoping without sense or reason.

Young man, do not run up bills which your riper years will find it hard to pay.

All means are to be used, notwithstanding the eternal purpose of God; for that purpose includes means and their uses.

If there be a commandment which you do not relish it ought to be a warning to you that there is something wrong in your heart that needs setting right.

When we rise again our nature will find its home amid the communion of saints. When the Lord Jesus Christ had risen again His first resort was the room where His disciples were gathered. His first evening was spent among the objects of His love. Even so, wherever we are we shall seek and find communion with the saints.

There is no good in sin in any shape or way.

Don't wait for helpers. Try those two old friends, your strong arms.

We ought never to go where we shall be out of the atmosphere of heaven.

Men who never smelt powder know exactly how a commander should have acted in a battle; probably they would themselves have run away at the first shot. Safely on land, the wiseacre decides most positively how the pilot should steer—which sail should be hoisted and which should be put away. If he were on board the laboring bark he would be lying down below, forgotten as a dead man out of mind.

Though sloth promises ease it cheats its votaries. Of all unrest there is none more wearisome than that of having nothing whatever to do.

"Whosoever" includes the slum people, even the poorest of the poor; but it does not exclude the carriage people; not even the richest of the rich. "Whosoever" beckons to the educated and looks favorably upon the cultured and the refined; but none the less does it invite the illiterate, to whom all learning is an unattainable mystery.

God prefers the prayer of a broken heart to the finest service that ever was performed by priests and choirs.

Heaven's long-suffering still runs like a silver thread through the centuries.

A thrifty housewife is better than a great income.

Self-consciousness is a sure sign that there is not much depth of grace.

The wide difference between wisdom and knowledge is forgotten by many; they hoard up knowledge of a peculiar sort like collectors of coins, and yet they use it not as merchants use money, but keep it for show, a rarity to be looked at, labeled, put away in a glass case, and exhibited to those who are admirers of curios and rarities.

Sin has been pardoned at such a price that we cannot henceforth trifle with it.

Some things being once done are done with, and you need not further meddle with them; but you have never done with rejoicing. "Rejoice ever more."

Perhaps you have lost the friendship of many by becoming disciples of the Lord Jesus. I know one who became a member of this church; she had moved in high and fashionable circles, but she said to me, "They have left me—every one of them." I said, "I am very thankful; for it will save you the trouble of quitting *them*. They will do you no good if they profess to be your friends; and they will do you less harm by giving you the cold shoulder."

Nothing is more mischievous than to cling to a name when the thing for which it stands has disappeared.

Lukewarmness of love to truth is the real evil to be deprecated in these times.

A man who becomes a great runner has to put himself in training and to keep himself in it; and that training consists very much of the exercise of running. Those who have distinguished themselves for speed have not suddenly leaped into eminence, but have long been runners. If a man dreams that he can become mighty in prayer just when he pleases he labors under a great mistake.

I must confess I never read the story of the Master's death, knowing what I do of the pain of crucifixion, without deep anguish.

To carry two faces under one hat is very common.

The deserts, where the sand is always shifting, where if the traveler once loses his bearings he is doomed to certain death, with the vulture's maw as his only sepulchre.

So many people have a "lean to" religion. If their minister, or some other leading person, were taken away, their back wall would be gone, and they would come to the ground. In some cases the wife and mother, or the husband and father, or the friend and teacher, constitute the main support of the individual's religion; he leans upon others, and if these fail him there is an end of his hope.

No man was ever yet found guilty of believing in God too much.

A man who knocks a horse about ought to be put in harness himself and be driven about.

Thoughts of heaven prevent discontent with our present lot.

However pleased the parents had been with the little one when it was a babe, they would soon be deeply distressed if year after year it still remained a tiny thing; indeed, they would consider it a great calamity to be the parents of a dwarf. What, then, shall we say of those in our churches who never grow? They are no forwarder after fifty years! Infants at sixty years of age!

It is a pity to pretend to predict the future, for we certainly cannot see an inch before us.

I believe that one of the sweetest joys under heaven comes out of the severest suffering when patience is brought into play.

There is not only an election from the world, but an election out of the elect. Twelve were taken from the disciples; three were taken out of the twelve; one greatly beloved was taken out of the three.

We believe in many conversions; we look for them, and we have them.

If your prayers have but few words in them, and are mainly made up of crying and tears, yet in this they are like those of your Saviour, and so you may hope that they will be accepted.

Trade with small capital means personal work and drudgery, long hours and few holidays, plenty of disappointment and small gains. It means working with might and main, and doing the thing with all your heart and mind.

Home is no home where the children are not in obedience; it is rather a pain than a pleasure to be in it.

Schemes of union are of small value; it is the spirit of union which is wanted.

Not even for the present are the reputations of the godly injured in the sight of God, and as for the future, they shall suffer no tarnishing. Soon there shall be a resurrection of good names as well as of bodies; the Lord shall restore the honor and renown of each slandered believer.

There is nothing more obnoxious to our divine Lord than distrust of Him.

It is often so to this day, that the servants of God smart because of disobedience. They are chastened for their sin.

Outward ordinances cannot secure a blessing; but the spirit of obedience, which leads to a careful observance of them according to the divine command, is a blessed fruit of the Spirit.

A hallowed influence lingers about the scenes of faithful labors.

Signing our petitions with the name Jesus! May we be importunate only in prayers to which we are warranted to set that august name; and then, boldly using His name and authority, we need be under no apprehension of failure.

I receive anything I ask for when I mention His name, and so I am sure that He is in wonderful high repute above.

As the seed develops into the flower, so the buried body is merely the germ out of which will come the spiritual body.

We ought to keep two bears, and learn to bear and forbear with one another.

The cares and labors of the day may carry the thoughts to other objects, even as a finger may turn the needle to the east or west, but no sooner is the pressure removed than the thoughts fly to the Well-Beloved just as the needle moves to its place.

We are not permitted to die at our own will. That were suicidal and improper.

In a little time—how little a time none of us can tell—we shall be where the inhabitant shall never be sick again. We are on our way to eternal health.

"The serpent's gospel," say you, "what is that?" It is another name for the gospel of modern thought—that gospel which casts a doubt upon the threatenings of the law and even denies them altogether.

That which is born with fear dies with fear.

One walking with me observed, with some emphasis: "I do not believe as you do. I am an Agnostic." "Oh," I said to him, "that is a Greek word, is it not? The Latin word, I think, is *ignoramus*." He did not like it at all. Yet I only translated his language from Greek to Latin.

Perfection lies in the observation of little things; and nothing is little by which a man can do a little good.

I'd rather walk ten miles to get out of a dispute than half a mile to get into one.

If we would not be run down by transgressors of one sort or another, we shall have need to be always on the watch.

Sin is as subtle and as deadly as the foul gas which bears within it the seeds of plague, and therefore the utmost caution must be used that we keep as far from its occasions and temptations as we possibly can.

We certainly should never fear death if we had no sin.

What is man's word compared with God's word? It is as chaff to the wheat at worst, and as mere gold-leaf to solid bullion at best.

If the tender mercy of God has visited us, and done so much more for us than I can tell or than you can hear, let us ourselves exhibit tender mercy in our dealings with our fellow-men.

Your tongue is too soft a thing to influence dull minds; you must influence such by your lives.

One book charmed us all the days of our youth. Is there a boy alive who has not read it? "Robinson Crusoe" was a wealth of wonders to me; I could have read it over a score of times and never have wearied. I am not ashamed to confess that I can read it even now with ever fresh delight.

The tendency to depreciate the present because of the glories of the past is injurious.

If a man is so proud that he will not see his faults he will only quarrel with you for pointing them out to him.

If any one says the four Gospels are forgeries, let him try to write a fifth, which shall be like the other four.

No wise man will swerve an inch from his path to please those who are mad with sin, nor will he break his heart because idiotic sinners make a jest of his uprightness.

He who will not go to the fire ought not to complain that the room is cold.

The religion of Jesus Christ acts upon truthful, reasonable, logical principles; *it is sanctified common sense.*

There is a laudable pursuit of gain without which business would not be properly carried on; but there is a line, scarcely as broad as a razor's edge, between diligence in business and greediness for gain.

Love is law; the law of love is the strongest of all laws.

The sin which at the first seemed a dainty luxury, sweet to their palate, has now developed into a corrosive poison in their bowels, eating their flesh as with fire, and burning up their spirits. Lust was their pilot; the siren of pleasure lured them on, and now they are wrecks, breaking into pieces on the rocks.

Christ's love is the sun and our love is the moonlight, which we are able to give forth because the sun hath looked upon us.

There are not so many hours in a year as there may be thoughts in an hour.

I think that it is always better to get the place quite full. It breeds a kind of enthusiasm.

When religion is at a discount and godliness is derided, then hypocrites and unsound professors desert the cause. It is astonishing what a little shake will get rid of the commonplace members of our churches.

Forgiveness begets gratitude, gratitude creates love, and love brings forth holiness.

The story of the great Lover of the souls of men, Who gave Himself for their salvation, is still, in the hand of the Holy Ghost, the greatest of all forces in the realm of mind.

Perhaps there is no greater soul-saving text in the Bible than this: "God so loved the world that He gave His only begotten Son, that whosoever believeth in Him should not perish, but have everlasting life." I must have conversed with more than a hundred persons who have found the Lord through this blessed verse. I am speaking very moderately, for I think I might say that I have known several hundreds who have been guided into liberty by *this pole-star text.*

There are no "ifs" where there is a God.

Boasters are never worth a button with the shank off.

In the shop of a diamond merchant at Amsterdam we saw great machinery and much power all brought to bear on what seemed to be a small piece of glass. One might be sure of the value of that transparent morsel if he would but look around and see what skill and labor were being expended upon it. God has laid out for the good of a soul the watchfulness of angels, the providence of this world, the glory of the next, the councils of eternity, Himself and all that He hath, the Holy Spirit and all his divine influences—yea, he spared not His only Son. Say, soul, what must thou be worth thus to have all heaven's thought and power and love laid out for thee?

There is no warmth like heart warmth, and no testimony like that of experience.

You have made up your mind about a great many things; unmake your mind, and be as wax to the seal before Him.

You scarcely meet with a man who will not acknowledge that he is a sinner. But it is one thing to call yourself a sinner, and quite another thing to feel it.

You are well aware that the division of the Bible into chapters has only been made for convenience sake, and is not a matter of inspired arrangement. I may add that it has been clumsily made, and not with careful thoughtfulness, but as roughly as if a woodman had taken an axe and chopped the book to pieces in a hurry.

The adversities of to-day are a preparatory school for the higher learning.

We have read that when Bernard visited a monastery of ascetic monks, they were shocked because the saddle on which he rode was most sumptuously adorned. They thought that this ill became his profession as a meek and lowly man. Judge of their surprise and satisfaction when he told them that he had never so much as noticed what it was whereon he sat. The fact was that the horse and saddle were not his own, but had been lent to him by his uncle, and their nature had not been perceived by him during the whole of his journey. This is the way to use all earthly treasure, making small account whether we have it or not.

Crucifixion was a death worthy to be invented by devils. The pain which it involved was immeasurable.

Our God has made the day-spring from on high to visit us. Our life is bright with these visits as the sky with stars.

Many hours in the day have to be spent upon our occupations. We wake up in the morning and think of what we have to do. We go to bed wearied at night by what we have done. This is as it should be, for God did not make us that we might sport and play like leviathan in the deep. Even in Paradise man was bidden to dress the garden. There is something to be done by each man, and specially by each Christian man.

Some are great liars, but they are hardly conscious of it; they have talked themselves into believing their own bombast.

The age of revival has had its men mighty in prayer.

He who respects his wife will find that she respects him.

God is not glorified by unused graces.

Experience has taught the wise observer that sin may be bound by sin, and one ruling passion may hold the rest in check. One man is kept from licentiousness by covetousness; he would be glad to revel in vice if it were not so expensive; another would be a rake and a spendthrift, but then it would not be respectable, and thus his pride checks his passions. This restraint of sin by sin is no proof that the nature is one jot the better, but that it puts on a fairer appearance, and is more likely to deceive.

He who overvalues himself undervalues his Saviour.

As the multitudes streamed forth from the hundred gates of Thebes, so do sins proceed from the heart.

The capacity to enjoy God, and to understand His superlative excellence, is the grandest faculty that a being can possess, and he that has it not is dead while he liveth.

Look at the many who died before we came into the world. Some of them have been in heaven together now for thousands of years. To them it must seem that they were only divided by a moment's interval; their continents of fellowship have made the channel of death seem but a streak of sea. Soon we shall take the same view of things.

If in the quiver of God's providence there should lie an arrow which shall to-day bring us death, it would also bring us glory.

A good wife and health are a man's best wealth.

The greatest worldly advantages cannot compensate for the loss of spiritual privileges.

Those who rejoice without knowing why can be driven to despair without knowing why.

Many processes are in vigorous action which tend to destroy faith.

If a man should labor to be rich after the African fashion, and should accumulate a large store of shells and beads, when he came home to England he would be a beggar, even though he had a ship-load of such rubbish. So he who gives his heart and soul to the accumulation of gold and silver coin is a beggar when he comes into the spiritual realm, where such round medals are reckoned as mere forms of earth, non-current in heaven, and of less value than the least of spiritual blessings.

The more we endure, the more we test the faithfulness of God, the more we prove His love, and the more we perceive His wisdom.

I shall enter into no dispute about the atoms of the body, nor deny that the particles of our flesh, in the process of their decay, may be taken up by plants and absorbed into the bodies of animals, and all that. I do not care one jot about identity of atoms; there may not be a solitary ounce of the same matter, but yet identity can be preserved; and it must be preserved if I read my Bible aright.

God sends every bird its food, but He does not throw it into the nest.

He who is making us ready for heaven is making heaven ready for us.

Those who play at the game of chess know that great circumspection is needed. Your opponent is working toward a design of which you know nothing, and while you imagine that you are doing exceedingly well he is entrapping you. The game of life, as against Satan, is one in which his age, his long practice, his superior skill, and his unscrupulousness give him an immense advantage over our poor self-conceited folly.

I am afraid that in the hour of our mirth and the day of our prosperity many of our prayers and our thanksgivings are hypocrisy.

The sinner who seeks to save himself by his own good works, or by any other means, toils without result. It is astonishing what pains men will take in this useless drudgery.

For a man to abstain from using force when he has none to use is no great virtue; it reminds one of the lines of Cowper's ballad:

> "Stooping down, as needs he must
> Who cannot sit upright."

But for a man to have force ready to his hand, and then to abstain from using it, is a case of self-restraint, and possibly of self-sacrifice, of a far nobler kind.

To injure another is worse by far than being injured ourselves.

If a man is ignorant and holds his tongue, no one will despise him.

Lord! help me to soar like the lark, but keep me clear of the net.

Business, marriage, traveling, recreation, literature, music, art, should all be placed in the same subordinate condition. They are not distinctly spiritual, and as mere human matters they may be either right or wrong; but it is ours to lay the yoke upon them and make them serve our spiritual designs. They will make admirable servants; we can never allow them to be our masters.

The Saviour offered no petitions by way of mere form; His supplications arose out of an urgent sense of His need of heavenly aid.

They that are not moral, they that are not honest, they that are not kind, they that are not truthful, are far from the kingdom. How can these be the children of God who are not even decent children of men?

Tarry here just a minute to recollect that the angels also are, according to your measure and degree, at your call. You have but to pray to God, and angels shall bear you up in their hands lest you dash your foot against a stone. We do not think enough of these heavenly beings; yet are they all ministering spirits sent forth to minister to those that are heirs of salvation.

A loveless religion is good for nothing.

Not those who pull the longest faces are the most in earnest.

If I had the option of my condition in life, I would rather have less earth and more heaven than more earth and less heaven.

We have seen the exhibitor turn away in utter disgust when some uninitiated spectator has offered pence where pounds would not have been accepted. The jeweler or artist has been as much offended as if he had been personally insulted by such a depreciation of his valuables. Do you wonder that the Lord God is grieved when men set a base price upon his priceless grace, and begin to bargain and chaffer as to what sins they will give up and what duties they will perform?

✓Sin is not a splash of mud upon man's exterior, it is a filth generated within himself.

Every church is to our Lord a more sublime thing than a constellation in the heavens; as He is precious to his saints, so are they precious to Him.

Because our Saviour's reasoning was unanswerable, "therefore the Jews sought again to take Him." When men are convinced against their wills, when the heart struggles against the head, it usually happens that they turn persecutors. If they cannot answer holy arguments with fair reasonings, they can give hard answers with stones.

There is a piety in keeping your work well in hand, in having the house right, the business in order, the daily task well done.

He has his money best spent who has the best wife.

Secret backslidings end in public abominations.

If we are out of temper ourselves, we plead the weather, or a headache, or our natural temperament, or aggravating circumstances; we are never at a loss for an excuse for ourselves. Why should not the same ingenuity be used by our charity in inventing apologies and extenuations for others?

We usually fear because we have cause for fear; when all is right we shall bid farewell to terror.

The joy which God commands is a joy in which it is impossible to go too far. It is a heavenly joy, based upon things which will last forevermore.

The raw material for a devil is an angel. The raw material for the son of perdition was an apostle; and the raw material for the most horrible of apostates is one who is almost a saint. I say no more than I mean, and than history can prove. There have usually been splendid traits of character about men who have been unfit to live.

If ever I have been satisfied with what I have done for the Lord I have ivnariably found my service to prove barren.

After the miser comes the prodigal.

Occupation is the remedy for many an internal sorrow.

A blind man may be a first-rate musician, and in his own department he may be a master, but if he ventures to dogmatize upon color and artistic portraiture he is more worthy of ridicule than of reverence. Carnal men have not the needful taste by which divine doctrine is discerned.

The Son is His glory, His darling, His *alter ego*, His other self—yea, one God with Him.

The thought of evil is sin; even a wanton desire is a blemish in the life, and an unchaste imagination is a stain upon the character in the sight of God, though not in the sight of man.

Perhaps you have almost taken it for granted that you love Jesus; but it must not be taken for granted. Some of you have been born in a religious atmosphere, you have lived in the midst of godly people, and you have never been out into the wicked world to be tempted by its follies; therefore you come to an immediate conclusion that you must assuredly love the Lord. This is unwise and perilous. I would have you fully assured of your love to Jesus, but I would not have you deceived by a belief that you love Him if you do not. Lord, search us and try us!

Faith travels by an unseen track to honor and glory, neither shall anything turn her aside.

Those who are helped in their better days generally forget the debt, or repay it with unkindness.

The presence of God is the only universal preservative.

Lord, whether I live long or not, I leave to Thee; but help me to live while I live that I may live much. Thou canst give life more abundantly; let me receive it, and let my life be filled, yea, packed and crammed, with all manner of holy thoughts and words and deeds to Thy glory.

Religion has cost many of its disciples somewhat dear; but it has cost nothing compared with its worth.

Trade develops a man's perseverance, patience, and courage; it tests honesty, truthfulness, and firmness. It is a singularly excellent discipline for character.

I will say broadly that I have more confidence in the spiritual life of the children that I have received into this church than I have in the spiritual condition of the adults thus received. I will even go further than that, and say that I have usually found a clearer knowledge of the Gospel and a warmer love to Christ in the child converts than in the man converts. I will even astonish you still more by saying that I have sometimes met with a deeper spiritual experience in children of ten and twelve than I have in certain persons of fifty and sixty.

God has made us, body and soul, and He would have us serve Him with both.

Depend upon it, plowing the air is not half so profitable as it is easy; he who hopes in this world for more than he can get by his own earnings hopes to find apricots on a crab-tree.

Neglect of prayer makes prayer become hard work.

Thou hast but little sunshine, but thy long glooms are wisely appointed thee, for perhaps a stretch of summer weather would have made thee as a parched land and a barren wilderness. Thy Lord knows best, and He has the clouds and the sun at His disposal.

He who prays aright with his heart will not much err with foot and hand and head.

Often it happens with those who try to get better by their own good works, that their conscience is awakened by the effort, and they are more conscious of sin than ever.

If you were to take out of the Scriptures all the stories that have to do with poor afflicted men and women, what a very small book the Bible would become, especially if together with the stories you removed all the psalms of the sorrowful, all the promises for the distressed, and all the passages which belong to the children of grief. This Book, indeed, for the most part is made up of the annals of the poor and despised.

Do not get to be so heavenly-minded that you cannot put up with the little vexations of the family.

All the neighbors are cousins to the rich man, but the poor man's brother does not know him.

Labor is lightened by being diversified.

A good wife does not sit idly by the sea watching for a sail, but she sets the house in order for her husband's return. She who sits looking out of the window or studying almanacs, and has no provision made for the homecoming, shows but scant love for her lord.

Be always true to your convictions about what Christ's commandments are. Carry them out at all hazards, and carry them out at once.

A doubtful faith will leave a doubt about your security; but those who believe out and out shall have joy and peace through believing.

Miserable professors who simply go to a place of worship because they ought to go, and who are very good because they dare not be anything else, they have no joy in the Lord. They go to the devil for their joy; they openly confess that they must have a bit of pleasure sometimes, and therefore they go to questionable amusements. No wonder that they are found in Satan's courts, looking up to him for delights, since they find no rejoicing in the ways of the Lord.

It is very seldom that a sluggard is honest; he owes at least more labor to the world than he pays.

Neither would I choose my lot on earth, but leave it with God to choose for me.

We shall never hear much pious conversation till we have more thorough conversions.

We give checks which are really nothing but pieces of paper made valuable by a man's name; and in the heaviest transactions of all, millions change from hand to hand without a coin being seen, the whole depending upon the honor and worth of those who sign their hands. What then? Shall not the Lord be trusted? Ay, with our whole being and destiny.

The encouragements of Christian communion are exceedingly great and the loss of them is very bitter.

I have known some very good people spoiled for practical usefulness and spoiled as to being like the Lord Jesus Christ by their deeply-laid conviction that it was wicked to be glad.

A person may happen to do you a good turn, but if you are sure that he did it by accident or with no more thought than that wherewith a passing stranger throws a penny to a beggar you are not impressed with gratitude; but when the action of your friend is the result of earnest deliberation and you see that he acts in the tenderest regard to your welfare you are far more thankful. Traces of anxiety to do you good are very pleasant. Do all things out of love, not for show.

A little word from a friend will pain you much more than a fierce slander from an enemy.

Horses are almost as hard to judge of as men's hearts; the oldest hands are taken in.

One of the nearest approaches to death is to be without thought.

Correcting for the press is work which has to be done with great care, since thousands of copies will be faulty if the proof-sheet be not as it should be. So should the minister of a congregation be seriously earnest to be right, because his people will imitate him. Like priest, like people; the sheep will follow the shepherd.

I should like those who think the salvation of souls from sin to be easy to try to convert one person.

Each day there is a judgment which, in God's apprehension, puts some upon the right hand with the "Come, ye blessed," and others upon the left hand with the "Depart, ye cursed." So many people (Christians et al.) who are more than anxious to accept God's right hand of righteousness, totally ignoring His left hand of justice.

Do not spin theories in your excited brains and vow that you will do this desperate thing and the other. The probability is that you are not seeking the glory of the Lord, but you are wanting notoriety for yourself. You are aiming at supreme devotion that you may become a distinguished person, and that people may talk about your superior saintship.

I fear that a terrible doom awaits those who go after the fashionable falsehoods of the day.

Eighteen pence has set up many a peddler in business, and he has turned it over till he has kept his carriage.

Great thoughts of self and great grace never go together.

The bee is our example, for she builds a house, but fetches all the material from abroad, and it is from the flowers of the garden and not from herself that she procures the honey with which she stores her cells. True believers get all the substance and sweetness of their hopes from the flowers of the promises, and dare not live upon themselves or anything that they can do or be.

Sin must be within us naturally, since the best training does not prevent it.

If one Christian man is right in never joining a Christian church, then all other Christian men would be right in not doing so, and there would be no visible Christian church.

Many very decent people are not self-contained, but are dependent upon the assistance of others. They are like the houses which our London builders run up so quickly in long rows; if they did not help to keep each other up they would all tumble down at once, for no one of them could stand alone. How much there is of joint-stock-company religion, wherein hypocrites and formalists keep each other in countenance.

I have seen the noblest character where the position was unfavorable.

Expect to get half of what you earn, a quarter of what is your due, and none of what you have lent, and you will be near the mark.

Better be dim gold than shining brass.

When we meet with persons of little substance but of considerable kindling power, let us put them together, like matches and splinters of wood, for the commencement of an enterprise, and when we find others to be like heavy old logs, let us put them to use when the flame has taken good hold, for if they once get thoroughly alight they will sustain the fire long after the straw and the shavings have passed away.

Have I not heard people say, "It was so kind and so thoughtful of him!" Do you not notice that men value kindly thought and set great store by tender consideration.

All men are sinners; to most men, however, sin appears to be a fashion of the times, a necessity of nature, a folly of youth, or an infirmity of age, which a slight apology will suffice to remove.

I say that this dying thief leads the van in the matter of faith, for what he saw of the circumstances of the Saviour was calculated to contradict rather than help his confidence. What he saw was to his hindrance rather than to his help, for he saw our Lord in the very extremity of agony and death, and yet he believed in Him as the King shortly to come into His kingdom.

Presence of mind is invaluable, and the best way to secure presence of mind is to believe in the presence of God.

God save us all from wives who are angels in the streets, saints in the church, and devils at home.

To lose sensitiveness of conscience is to lose the excellence of our being.

Brambles certainly have a fine time of it, and grow after their own pleasure. We have seen their long shoots reaching far and wide, and no knife has threatened them as they luxuriated upon the commons and waste lands. The poor vine is cut down so closely that little remains of it but bare stems. Yet, when clearing-time comes, and the brambles are heaped for their burning, who would not rather be the vine.

How many hearts mightest thou have won for thy Lord if thine own heart had been fuller of love, if thine own soul had been more on fire!

Nobody speaks so sternly against sin as Jesus and those who believe His gospel; but yet it forever stands true, "This man receiveth sinners."

There is a passage in the Psalms which makes the Lord do for us what one would have thought we could have done for ourselves—"He maketh me to lie down in green pastures." Surely, if a sheep can do nothing else it can lie down. Yet, to lie down is the very hardest thing for God's sheep to do. It is here that the full power of the rest-giving Christ has to come in to make our fretful, worrying, doubtful natures lie down and rest.

When the Spirit of God works with your persuasions your convert will keep His pledge.

The thought that we may ourselves be one day under the window should make us careful when we are throwing out our dirty water.

The Gospel, the whole Gospel, and nothing but the Gospel, must be our religion or we are lost men.

No one fights with a statue, but living soldiers are often in the wars; living Christians are sure to be assailed in one way or another, Let us therefore for once gather figs of thistles, and find comfortable fruit upon the thorns and briers of persecution. The world is no fool; it would not be so fierce against us if it did not see something about us contrary to itself; its enmity, therefore, is part evidence that we are the children of God.

Every man should labor by precept and example to put down intemperance.

If a church labors to keep the ordinances as they were delivered, and endeavors to follow in the track of Christ's teaching and example, it may hope to receive the divine blessing.

How many who only meant to go a little from the old ways of truth have gone too far aside even for themselves! Truly, my speculative friend, "Thy rowers have brought thee into great waters." I am not intending to follow you. You are so wise that I am satisfied to be a fool, because I would wish to be the reverse of what you are.

You little know what a tyrant he serves who lives as he lists.

"Why," says one, "I think John would get a new wife if he were left a widower." Well, and what if he did; how could he better show that he was happy with his first? I declare I would not say, as some do, that they married to have some one to look after the children; I should marry to have some one to look after myself.

If we indulge a sin we invite a sorrow.

Stagnation in business, pressure for money, and the temptation to speculate fetch down many rotten Christians. The fashion of the world, the luxuries of life, and the habits of wealthy society also shake off others from their visible profession.

To believe in the notion of a God is one thing, but to believe God is quite another matter.

If men did but more carefully watch their thoughts they would not so readily fall into evil habits; but men first indulge the thought of evil and then the imagination of evil.

When we shall rise again from the dead we shall remember the past. Do you not notice how the risen Saviour says, "These are the words which I spake unto you while I was yet with you." He had not forgotten His former state. It is rather a small subject, and probably we shall far more delight to dwell on the labors of our Redeemer's hands and feet; but still we shall remember all the way whereby the Lord our God led us, and we shall talk to one another concerning it. In heaven we shall remember our happy Sabbaths here below, when our hearts burned within us while Jesus himself drew near.

Well may we be a nation of beggars if we are a nation of drinkers.

Eggs are eggs, but some are rotten; and so hopes are hopes, but many of them are delusions. Hopes are like women, there is a touch of angel about them all—but there are two sorts.

There is never a pause in our progress toward eternity.

Till Jesus communed with me I did not know that I could be so happy. I heard more birds singing in my soul than I ever dreamed could have dwelt within me. Never had my sad soul imagined that human life was half as capable of divine bliss or earth within a thousand leagues so near to heaven.

Let us despise all pride of birth, rank, or wealth; therefore speak no more so exceedingly proudly. It is madness for dying men to boast.

Heaven on earth is abounding love to Jesus. This is the first and last of true delight—to love Him who is the first and the last. To love Jesus is another name for paradise.

To me it is a solemn memory that I professed my faith openly in baptism. Vividly do I recall the scene. It was the third of May, and the weather was cold because of a keen wind. I see the broad river, and the crowds which lined the banks, and the company upon the ferry-boat. The word of the Lord was preached by a man of God who is now gone home; and when he had so done, he went down into the water, and we followed him, and he baptized us. I remember how, after being the slave of timidity, I rose from the liquid grave quickened into holy courage by that one act of decision, consecrated henceforth to bear a life-long testimony. By an avowed death to the world I professed my desire henceforth to live with Jesus, for Jesus, and like Jesus.

We can be good workers for the Lord and successful fruit-bearers for his glory without having the pick of places.

Show me a loving husband, a worthy wife, and good children, and no pair of horses that ever flew along the road could take me in a year where I could see a more pleasing sight.

The new birth has disqualified us for contentment with the world.

We cannot think of our sin without grieving, and the more sure we are that it is forgiven, the more sorry we are that ever it was committed.

It is the old-fashioned, quiet, personal work which is effectual. If we get to think that everything must be big to be good, we shall get into a sorry state of mind.

It is a sad thing for any sort of people when Jesus can say of them, "Verily, I say unto you, *they have* their reward." They cannot expect to be paid twice, and as their account is discharged in full, what have they to look for?

I used, as a youth, sometimes to think that I was as good as other lads, and perhaps I was, for I had not fallen into the grosser vices. I fancied that if anybody was saved by a moral life, I might be. But oh, when God lifted the veil of my nature, and I saw what my heart really was, I sang to another tune. I had been down into the cellar of my heart a great many times in the dark, and it seemed pretty fair; but when the Holy Spirit opened the shutters and let in the light, what loathsome abomination I saw there. My life, too, no longer appeared to be the goodly thing I had imagined it. Ah! no, my comeliness was turned into corruption.

Our Lord is grieved for us when he sees us fall so low that, instead of being like Himself, we are not even like ourselves.

The 'squire can be heard for half a mile if he only whispers, but Widow Needy is not heard across the park railings, let her call as she may.

With difficulty can a man prevent the world's influencing him for evil.

We sometimes think too exclusively of salvation as having reference to the world to come; but it has an urgent, all-important reference to this present state.

The Lord has some of His children whose heads are in a very queer state; and if He first puts their hearts right He will afterward put their heads right.

Here is a little child picked from the gutter; it is starved, unclothed, unwashed, and sickening to death. What does it want? Well, it would take me a long time to write out a list of all its wants. It needs washing, clothing, warming, feeding, nursing, loving—no, I will not attempt to complete the catalogue, but I will tell you all in a word: this little child wants *its mother*. If it finds a loving and capable mother, it has all that it needs at once. Every lost soul of man needs a thousand things; but no soul needs more than it will find in God.

It is not uncharitable to warn men against poisonous adulterations of their food or invasions of their rights; and surely it cannot be more uncharitable to put them upon their guard against that which will poison or rob their souls.

Choicest of all forms of power—the power of prayer.

Cobblers have turned their lapstones into gold.

The price of love is love.

If called in poverty to sing bass, blessed is he who sings so as to please the ear of God; he shall be fully as accepted as his neighbor who exalts his voice upon a higher key. So long as the music of his life is true to the score of duty, no man will be censured because his notes were not so strong, or high, or many as those of another in the company.

The motive-power of action to a believing man lies hard by the realization that God, for Christ's sake, hath forgiven his iniquities.

Live so that you need not change your mode of living, even if your sudden departure were immediately predicted to you. When you so live you will look upon death without fear.

Sudden conversions have not ceased. I knew a man, a singular person, but a sincere Christian, who, in his early days, never thought of going to any place of worship. One Sunday morning he set out to visit a comrade, intending to conclude a bargain which had been talked over the day before, *about a pair of ducks*. He stepped into the meeting-house because it came on to rain, and there he found what he had never sought. He never bought that pair of ducks; he forgot them, as the woman of Samaria forgot her water-pot. The Lord met with him there and then, and he beheld his Saviour.

It is down in your diary in black and white that His mercy endureth forever.

Thousands ruin themselves by idle expectations.

A man may dream that he is among the stars, and may suddenly wake to find that he has battered his face against the post of his bed; dreaming, doting, and theorizing are poor substitutes for "real" experience of divine things.

It is with the transgressor as with the falling stone, the further he falls the faster he falls.

Our hope is that we shall be approved of Him, and shall hear Him say: "Well done, good and faithful servant."

A man who does not know Christ is a wretched man; a man who has never been renewed in heart, who lives in sin and loves it, is a pitiable being, a lost soul over whom angels might weep.

As for myself, I know that I was born in sin, and I know that in me—that is, in my flesh—there dwelleth no good thing. I know also that I once tried to purge and cleanse my own heart, and labored at it, I believe, as honestly as any person that lived. I went about to seek a righteousness of my own, and I endeavored to get quit of sin; but my failure was complete. I do not advise any other person to try self-healing. It brought me to despair; it drove me almost to the loss of reason. Therefore speak I of my own experience; and, taught by my own failure, I cannot urge any man to seek cleansing by his own doings or efforts, but I urge him to accept that cleansing which God has promised in the covenant of grace.

Some trumpets are so stuffed with self that God cannot blow through them.

If I had no home the world would be a big prison to me.

The Lord himself teaches us to judge what our Heavenly Father will do for us by that which we would do for our children.

Secret reservoirs, far up in the mountains, supply the water-springs; and eternal deeps of boundless love in the everlasting hills supply the love-springs of the believer's soul. Is it not written, "All my fresh springs are in thee?"

If men are not warned of the anger of God against iniquity they will take license to riot in evil.

We crave the world, we sigh for human approbation, we seek for ease and comfort, we desire above all things to indulge our pride with the vain notion of self-righteousness.

It would seem that there is no worse abuse of a good thing than to abstain from its use.

Paul knew but little of the world, except that portion of it which bordered on the Mediterranean Sea; the whole world then seemed to lie in a nutshell; but now our discoverers and geographers, our steamboats and telegraphs, have brought a greater world close to our doors. We share with the sorrows of India; we groan in the darkness of Africa; the cries of China are at our doors, and Egypt's griefs are our own. Increase of knowledge demands increase of prayer.

He promised to come to die, and He kept His word; He now promises to come to reign, and be you sure that He will keep His tryst with His people.

All the world will beat the man whom fortune buffets.

A man had better have the prince for a friend than possess a thousand images of the king, his father, upon gold and silver; and so it is a happier thing for us to know that Christ is ours than to possess all other blessings, however much of God there may be about them.

Our lives through various scenes are drawn and vexed with petty provocations. Paltry annoyances are the bane of our peace.

In vain you boast the enlightenment of this nineteenth century; the nineteenth century is not one whit more enlightened as to the depravity of human nature than the first century.

The world is not going to darken into an eternal night; the morning cometh as well as the night, and though sin and corruption abound, and the love of many waxeth cold, these are but the tokens of His near advent who said that it would be so before His appearing. The right with the might and the might with the right shall be; as surely as God lives, it shall be so. We are not fighting a losing battle. The Lord must triumph.

It is a pity to take much notice of what some sufferers say, for they will be sorry for it soon.

They who join their love in God above, who pray to love and love to pray, will find that love and joy will never cloy.

To be holy and gracious needs many a struggle, many a tear.

All the sea outside a ship cannot do it damage till the water enters within and fills the hold. Hence, it is clear, our greatest danger is from within. All the devils in hell and tempters on earth could do us no injury if there were no corruption in our nature.

If there is one who is servant to that black master I would recommend him to run to Christ and not give his master five minutes' notice.

He who protests against a self-righteous people, and angers them by showing that others whom they despised are saved while they themselves are being lost, will have need of a dauntless spirit.

One of the commandments of the saints of misery is: "Draw down the blinds on a Sunday." Another is: "Never smile during a sermon; it is wicked." A third precept is: "Never rest yourself, and be sure that you never let anybody else rest for an instant. Why should anybody be allowed a moment's quiet in a world so full of sin? Go through the world and impress people with the idea that it is an awful thing to live."

The ideal Christian is one who has been made alive with a life which he lives for God.

Some men can neither do without wives nor with them; they are wretched alone in what is called single blessedness, and they make their homes miserable when they get married.

Contentment is the crown jewel of a happy life.

If we would please God we must watch every stroke and touch upon the canvas of our lives, and we may not think that we can lay it on with a trowel and yet succeed. We ought to live as miniature painters work, for they watch every line and tint.

He that is truly great among men is tender, because he is great in heart as well as in brain and hand.

Like Paul, have a strong desire to depart and to be with Christ, and yet be willing to wait if we can do service to our Lord and to His Church.

Independence and a clear conscience are better with cold cabbage than slavery and sin with roast beef.

The officers were after our Lord, and He knew it. He could spy them out in the crowd, but He was not therefore in the least afraid or disconcerted. He reminds me of that minister who, when he was about to preach, was stopped by a soldier, who held a pistol at his head and threatened that if he spake he would kill him. "Soldier," said he, "do your duty; I shall do mine;" and he went on with his preaching. The Saviour, without saying as much in words, said so by His actions.

Friendship is one of the sweetest joys of life; many spirits might have failed beneath the bitterness of trial if they had not found a friend.

Those who disdain to live for God will live for their own bellies.

A man's handwriting binds him. Now, we may be sure that the Lord will never deny his own writing nor run back from a bond given under his own hand and seal. Every promise of Scripture is a writing of God, which may be pleaded before Him with this reasonable request: "Do as Thou hast said."

No man hears his pastor preach without deriving some benefit from him, if he has earnestly prayed for him.

Cast your eye over every land, glance from the pole to the equator, and along to the other pole, and see if this be not the universal law, that man must be dissolved in death.

Still further to confirm the faith of the disciples, and to show them that their Lord had a real body, and not the mere form of one, He gave them evidence which appealed to their common sense. He said, "Have ye any meat? And they gave Him a piece of broiled fish, and of an honey-comb. And He took it, and did eat before them." This was an exceedingly convincing proof of his unquestionable resurrection. In very deed and fact, and not in vision and phantom, the man who had died upon the cross stood among them.

Not much good comes of picking holes in other men's characters, and yet many spend hours in that unprofitable occupation.

Success is the crucible of character.

When home is ruled according to God's word, angels might be asked to stay a night with us, and they would not find themselves out of their element.

If we look for Christ to come we shall keep our eyes heavenward and our minds occupied with the country from which He cometh. If we mind earthly things it will be evidence that the coming of the Lord has no power over us.

Dear young fellow, you may be turned out of your situation, but the Lord will turn the curse into a blessing.

I believe that great holiness sets us free from the love of this world and makes us ready to depart. By great holiness I mean great horror of sin and great longing after perfect purity.

The Church is the bride of Christ, and for a bride to fail in love is to fail in all things. It is idle for the wife to say that she is obedient, and so forth; if love to her husband has evaporated, her wifely duty cannot be fulfilled; she has lost the very life and soul of the marriage state. So, my brethren, this is a most important matter, our love to Christ, because it touches the very heart of that communion with Him which is the crown and essence of our spiritual life. As a church, we must love Jesus or else we have lost our reason for existence. Lose love, lose all. Leave our first love, we have left strength and peace and joy and holiness.

No character like that of Jesus is to be seen in history—nay, not even in romance.

If there's one bad shilling taken at the grocer's all the neighbors hear of it, but of the hundreds of good ones report says nothing.

The gentleness of Christ is a choice qualification for a pastor.

It is a blessed thing to think of heaven at the end; but it is an almost equally blessed thing to think of God with us on the way.

It is not necessary for a person's life for him to know where he was born; yet I am glad that I know my birthplace, and I am happy to remember the humble spot.

The assaults of sceptics are a gain to believers, for they produce a clearing and opening up of the truth. Opposition directs attention to neglected doctrines, and heresy calls for orthodox replies, and so our defenses become stronger as our enemies become more furious.

God has *many very naughty children;* they fall into quarrels with their Heavenly Father. "Ever since that dear child died," says one, "I have never felt the same toward God." "Ever since my mother was taken away," cries another, "I have always felt that I could not trust God as I used to do." This is shocking talk. Have done with it. If you quarrel with God, He will say to you, "It is hard for thee to kick against the pricks." There is no happiness but in complete submission. Yield, and all will end well; but if you stand out against the Most High, it is not God's rod that makes you smart; it is a rod of your own making. End this warfare by saying, "It is the Lord; let Him do what seemeth to Him good." Do not say, "He blessed me up to a certain point, and then He changed His hand." This is a most slanderous falsehood.

Depend upon it, those useful workers whom you so much envy have their private griefs, which minister to their usefulness or keep them humble under their success.

No man's lot is fully known till he is dead; change of fortune is the lot of life.

We are more forcible in communicating sin than virtue.

Often does it happen that the boaster is tripped up by the enemy whom he thought to be dead and buried, while the watchful, careful Christian is preserved in the midst of the fiercest temptations and enabled to maintain his integrity.

The devil's work is never done; it is undone again in five minutes when the grace of God is at work.

The possibilities of a man are stupendous. God with a man, nothing is impossible to that man. Give us not the power of gold, or rank, or eloquence, or wisdom, but give us a man.

There is more satisfaction in Christ's worst things than in sin's best things.

I have preached His Gospel now for many years, but I never met with a sinner yet that Christ refused to cleanse when he came to Him. I never knew of a single case of a man who trusted Jesus, and asked to be forgiven, confessing his sin and forsaking it, who was cast out. I say I never met with one man whom Jesus refused; nor shall I ever do so. I have spoken with harlots whom He has restored to purity, and drunkards whom he has delivered from their evil habit, and with men guilty of foul sins who have become pure and chaste through the grace of our Lord Jesus. They have always told me the same story—"I sought the Lord, and He heard me; He hath washed me in His blood and I am whiter than snow."

How many thousands have there been of true helpmeets, worth far more than their weight in gold! There is only one Job's wife mentioned in the Bible and one Jezebel, but there are no end of Sarahs and Rebekahs.

If there be no growth, it may be, nay, surely it must be, that you are not a child born into the family of God, but a pretty picture, which may adorn a room, but which cannot perform any of the actions of life.

As I conceive the face of Christ, it was very different from anything that any painter has yet been able to place upon his canvas.

That man who feels a daily striving after deliverance from evil, who is panting, and pining, and longing, and agonizing to become holy even as God is holy, he is the justified man.

Surely, if at any period in our lives we should consider our latter end it is when the frail tent of our body begins to tremble because the cords are loosened and the curtain is rent. It is the general custom with sick people to talk about "getting well," and those who visit them, even when they are gracious people, will see the tokens of death upon them, and yet will speak as if they were hopeful of their recovery. I remember a father asking me when I prayed with a consumptive girl to be sure not to mention death. In such cases it would be far more sensible for the sick man to turn his thoughts towards eternity, and stand prepared for the great change.

When a meteor darts across the sky children say that a star has fallen, but it is not so. So, too, we hear men say that a Christian has fallen from grace, a saint has become an apostate. This also is an error. The saints are in their places still, for it is written, "the righteous shall hold on his way;" those who have fallen were meteors, not stars; professors, but not genuine possessors of the heavenly light. The seven stars are in a hand out of which nothing falls: "All the saints are in thy hand." Jesus says, "He that believeth in me hath everlasting life," and therefore we are sure that they will not die.

Friends ever have an ear for friends.

Beware of those who come from the town of Deceit.

It is no time for boasting while we are still in the enemy's country.

The race forgets its masters but it remembers its friends.

It is easier to get a sinner out of his sin than a self-righteous man out of his self-righteousness.

Nobody will err about the way to God if he really resolves to follow that way. The Spirit of God will guide those whose hearts are set upon coming to God.

I asked a question some years ago of a person whom I believed to be one of the most covetous individuals in my acquaintance, and I received from him a singular reply. I said: "How was it that St. Francis de Sales, who was an eminent confessor, to whom persons went in the Romish Church to confess their sins, found that persons confessed to him in private all sorts of horrible sins, such as adultery, drunkenness, and murder, but never had one person confessed the sin of covetousness?" I asked this friend whether he could tell me why it was, and he made me this answer, which certainly did take me rather aback. He said: "I suppose it is because *the sin is so extremely rare.*" Blind soul! I told him that, on the other hand, I feared the sin was so very common that people did not know when they were covetous, and that the man who was most covetous of all was the last person to suspect himself of it.

The worst foes of the truth are not infidels, but false professors.

Economy is a fine thing, and makes nine pence go further than a shilling.

Where avarice is the absolute master, the man is a miser.

We have heard persons talk of the days of childhood as the happiest in mortal life, but we do not agree with them; the sorrows of childhood take a very intense possession of the little ones, and in their grief everything seems lost, whereas the full-grown mind is divided in sorrow, and other considerations come in to temper the wind of trouble.

The service of the world is much sterner, much more exacting, much more wearisome, than the service of the Lord Jesus Christ.

The most horrible thing in the world is for a man no longer to be able to speak with his Maker, nor his Maker to look favorably upon him.

In heaven the saints will be nearer to Christ than the apostles were when they sat at the table with Him or heard Him pray. That was a nearness which might consist only in place, and their minds might still be, as they often were, far away from Him; but up in heaven we shall be one with Him in sympathy, in spirit, in conscious fellowship.

Power to do good involves the duty of doing good.

When the devil sees hypocrites at their little game it must be as good as a play to him; he tempts genuine Christians, but he lets these alone, because he is sure of them.

Old men are not always wise men.

Satan first acts as deceiver and then as accuser. While men can be made to suck down sin he will make it sweet in their mouths; but when the poison is down he makes it bitter in their bowels. At the first he tells them that there is no punishment, and by and by that there is no mercy.

I always have a warm side toward odd, eccentric, out-of-the-way people, because I am one myself—at least, so I am often said to be.

We cannot all of us praise God in the family by joining in song, because we are not all able to raise a tune, but it would be well if we could.

By your anxious care you may seek to detain them; you may sit about their bed and nurse them both night and day, but they must quit these dark abodes when Jesus gives the signal. You may clutch them with affectionate eagerness, and even cry in despair, "They shall not go, we cannot bear to part with them;" but go they must when Jesus calls.

Friendship, if it exists, will breed mutual delight.

I've known men who open their mouths like barn doors in boasting what they would do if they were in somebody's else shoes.

Every saint taken home brings the world so much nearer its end.

Few knit out of the many flowers which make promise of apples. It has ever been so, and he is an unwise man who dreams that his trees will be exempted from the universal law. The same rule holds good in all earthly matters. Out of many hopeful results which we look for from our plans and labors, some must fail us.

Snails leave their slime behind them, and so do vain thoughts.

Let us make worldlings know the fragrance of our joyous hope; especially let us tell those who seem most likely to laugh at us, for we have learned by experience that some of these are most likely to be impressed.

This Bible is our treasure. We prize each leaf of it. Let us bind it in the best fashion, in the best morocco of a clear, intelligent faith; then let us put a golden clasp upon it, and gild its edges by a life of love, and truth, and purity, and zeal. Thus shall we commend the volume to those who have never looked within its pages.

Either give up sin or give up hope.

A well-matched couple carry a joyful life between them. They multiply their joys by sharing them, and lessen their troubles by dividing them; this is fine arithmetic.

As a lamp is all the more valued when the night is dark, so is the Gospel all the more precious when men see their misery without it.

This we know by experience: Sweet is the music of the English tongue when heard amid the clatter of foreign speech. We feel our heart warmed at the sight of a costume which we can recognize as covering a true Briton. Such are the feelings of a Christian when he falls in with a true believer, and by his speech and conduct knows him to be a citizen of heaven.

A frightened sinner is a sinner still.

If you and I felt our Lord's anxiety to be serving God and winning souls, we should find refreshment in the service itself, even as He did.

For that Revised Version I have but little care, as a general rule, holding it to be by no means an improvement upon our common Authorized Version. It is a useful thing to have it for private reference, but I trust it will never be regarded as the standard English translation of the New Testament. The Revised Version of the Old Testament is so excellent that I am half afraid it may carry the Revised New Testament upon its shoulders into general use. I sincerely hope that this may not be the case, for the result would be a decided loss.

The Gospel is that God hath mercy upon the guilty and undeserving.

The dog wags his tail till he gets the bone, and then he snaps and bites at the man who fed him.

Perseverance in prayer is necessary to prevalence in prayer.

See how men throw overboard the lading of the ship when it becomes a question of saving their lives. Reason teaches them that the less precious must go first; they do not throw over first their gold and then their corn, neither do they lose their lives to save their ingots. So let us, above all things, care for our souls and their eternal interests.

May our life work close as sets the sun, looking greater when he sinks into the west than when he shines at full meridian height!

No doubt by praying we learn to pray, and the more we pray the oftener we can pray, and the better we can pray.

Two men alone entered the next world without seeing death, but those two exceptions prove the rule. Another great exception is yet to come, which I would never overlook. Peradventure the Lord Jesus Christ may personally come before we see death, and when He cometh we that are alive and remain shall not fall asleep; but even then "We shall all be changed in a moment, in the twinkling of an eye, at the last trump; for the dead shall be raised incorruptible, and we shall be changed."

Satan assails us through our fellows.

Fine dressing makes a great hole in poor people's means.

God has laid no embargo upon rejoicing; He puts no restriction upon happiness. Do believe it that you are permitted to be happy.

A believer may be truly alive unto God, though by his carelessness he has lost all the wealth of the spiritual life, and has fallen into soul poverty. Such a man should not despair, but with deep humiliation he should begin again. A tradesman who has failed will take to a humble calling to earn his bread, and so should a Christian who has broken down in his spiritual estate take a lowly position, and with all diligence labor to glorify the Lord better than before.

Trust in self is a disloyal attempt upon the crown rights of the Redeemer. All those doings and willings and feelings are a setting up of self-salvation.

I have on several occasions felt everything like fear of dying taken from me simply by the process of weariness; for I could not wish to live any longer in such pain as I then endured.

Despite our ignorance, nothing can go wrong while the Lord in infinite knowledge ruleth over all. The child playing on the deck does not understand the tremendous engine whose beat is the throbbing heart of the stately Atlantic liner, and yet all is safe; for the engineer, the captain, and the pilot are in their places and well know what is being done. Let not the child trouble itself about things too great for it.

Warm-hearted saints keep each other warm.

Lewd words soon lead to foul deeds.

A great deal of water can be got from a small pipe if the bucket is always there to catch it.

In the world to come the ceaseless activity of conscience will be the torture of hell. Rendered sensitive by the removal of hardening influences, the lost soul will find memory accusing and conscience condemning forever, and no advocate at hand to suggest a defense. A man had better be shut up with a bear robbed of her whelps than live with an accusing conscience. No racks or fires can equal the misery of being consciously guilty and seeing no way of escape from sin.

In dark mines men find bright jewels, and so from our worst troubles come our best blessings.

Practical doing is better than loud boasting.

There is a joy in achieving a great purpose, even when it is only by sorrow that our design is wrought out.

The way to make men better is not to be always censuring them, but to love them better.

We may speak of sleeplessness very lightly, but among afflictions it is one of the worst that can happen to men.

To this life of yours and mine there can be no postscript. We must do our work now or never.

The further a man goes in lust and iniquity the more dead he becomes to purity and holiness; he loses the power to appreciate the beauties of virtue or to be disgusted with the abominations of vice.

I hardly know of a more conscious union between a man and Christ than that which is effected when in sinking times the grip of the crucified hand is felt as our sole rescue from death.

Before we rebuke another we must consider and take heed that we are not guilty of the same thing, for he who cleanses a blot with inky fingers makes it worse.

Be half a Christian and you shall have enough religion to make you miserable; be wholly a Christian and your joy shall be full.

Blessed is that man who never deliberates, because his mind is made up rather to "suffer affliction with the people of God than to enjoy the pleasures of sin for a season."

I have noticed old people whose memories have been sadly feeble. I knew one who forgot his children. But I never knew an old saint yet who forgot the name of the Saviour or failed to remember His love.

Certain things that you and I may do may appear right, and yet we may need to be chidden out of them into something better; they may be right in themselves, but not appropriate for the occasion, not seasonable, nor expedient.

At this present moment there is a place in heaven for me that nobody can ever fill but my own self; and Jesus has gone before, not only to prepare it, but to prepare it *for me.* There is a crown that no head but mine can ever wear and a song that no tongue but mine can ever sing, and I shall soon cast my crown at Jesus' feet and chant before Him my hallelujahs. That is true of every believer.

The sermon that only gets as far as the ear is like a dinner eaten in a dream.

Sin has this mischief about it, that it strikes a man with spiritual paralysis.

He will save even you, though you are as bad as you well can be.

If I were to try and tell all the things that make Christians glad, even here below, I should have to make an endless catalogue.

He seeth not as man seeth, with a mere gaze of cold notice; but His heart goes with his eye.

I find it forbidden in Scripture for any man to call his brother "fool," but I do not find him forbidden to call himself so.

No pace is too swift for God to come to the deliverance of His people. He is slow to anger, but He is swift in mercy.

Truth is like those crystals which, when split up into the smallest possible fragments, still retain their natural form.

"The Man of Joys!" I venture thus to name the Christ of God. We do not often enough meditate upon the happiness of the Lord Jesus Christ.

Surely it ill becomes us to waste a penny, an hour, or an opportunity. Let us be severely economical for the Lord our God.

Anger does a man more hurt than that which made him angry. It opens his mouth and shuts his eyes and fires his heart and drowns his sense and makes his wisdom folly.

Those who preach not the atonement exhibit a dumb and dummy gospel; a mouth it hath and speaketh not; they that make it are like unto their idol.

I cannot imagine a fuller present reward than complete rest from all anxiety and calm confidence in a Providence which can never fail.

However much the Church may have been increased by a true revival, God has never as yet done according to the fullness of His ability in the Church; even Pentecost was but the first-fruits.

If we greatly grow in faith it will be the source of other growths; for as faith increases, love, patience, and every other virtue will flourish.

I have known many in this world very loving and affectionate, but they have not been faithful; on the other hand, I have known men to be sternly honest and truthful, but they have not been gentle and kind; but in the Lord Jesus Christ there is no defect either way.

Some things want doing gently, and telling a man of his faults is one of them.

Blessed are they who do what they should do.

Sin multiplies itself very rapidly.

Some are hindered in their usefulness by their great dignity. In many, dignity is a mask for pride & supposed superiority.

Sin is in itself an unmitigated evil, a root which beareth wormwood.

Where spiritual life is weak it should be nurtured with affectionate care.

God's errands are so important that we must not delay in their performance.

Silent acts of love have musical voices in the ear of Jesus.

It is not the box that makes the jewel, nor the place that makes the man.

Deep as were His griefs, we may reckon Jesus of Nazareth among the happiest of men.

Prayer is the autograph of the Holy Ghost upon the renewed heart.

I am always afraid of the tail end of a habit. A man who is always in debt will never be cured till he has paid the last sixpence.

Our circumstances compel us to think of lower objects, but we need divine help to abide in communion with the higher matters.

As Peter's fish had the money in its mouth, so have sanctified trials spiritual riches for those who endure them graciously.

We should not know ourselves if we could see ourselves as we are to be when the Lord's purpose is accomplished upon us.

Two little words are good for every Christian to learn and to practice—pray and stay. Waiting on the Lord implies both praying and staying.

If there is but a step between you and death—if the Judge is at the door—go and wind up your little difficulties. You that have family quarrels, wipe them out. You that have any malice in your heart, turn it out.

Trials are like a fire; they burn up nothing in us but the dross, and they make the gold all the purer. Put down the testing process as a clear gain, and, instead of being sorry about it, count it all joy when you fall into divers trials, for this bestows upon you a proof of your faith.

Prating does not make saints, or there would be plenty of them.

A man that lives without prayer ought not to live.

Starve your soul and you will be wretched amid the dainties of a king's table.

A true disciple is a follower; he is an imitator of his Master. Choose your Master well.

There is as much real practice about right thinking as about right acting.

We associate with His crucifixion much of sorrowful regret, but we derive from His birth at Bethlehem nothing but delight.

Do let us try with all our hearts so to look every man upon the things of others that no single seeking soul shall feel itself deserted.

The terrible acts of the Lord are few, but no age is quite left without them, for the Lord liveth still, and He is evermore the same. Yesterday – Today & Tomorrow!

It is as easy to make an idol out of your own thoughts as it is for the Hindoo to make a god of the mud of the Ganges.

The Lord will allow no service to remain unrecompensed; and work done for the poor and needy shall win its wage, not of debt, but of grace.

A man who cannot push on against wind and weather stands a poor chance in this world.

The Lord's providence rules words as well as deeds, and makes men say the right words without their knowing why they say them.

If you once hear the Gospel you can never be indifferent to it; you must either be its friend or its foe, its disciple or its opposer.

Prosperity softens and renders us unfit for more of itself, but adversity braces the soul and hardens it to patience.

Prayer is the outcome of that sense of need which arises from the new life; a man would not pray to God if he did not feel that he had urgent need of blessings which only the Lord can bestow.

Though the dollar is not almighty, it ought to be used *for* the Almighty and not wasted in wicked extravagance.

Afflictions by God's grace make us *all-round men*, developing every spiritual faculty, and therefore they are our friends, our helpers, and should be welcomed with "all joy."

I call that man a fool who throws away jewels that he may gather pebbles, who casts away gold and silver that he may gather up mire and dirt. And what do they do who fling away heaven and eternal life for the sake of a transient joy, a momentary gain?

That which we do to display our own liberality is done unto self, and so is spoiled.

There is something very beautiful about that which is done by new converts.

The work of pressed men is never so much prized as that of happy volunteers.

Christianity has a great uniting power; it both discovers and creates relationships among the sons of men.

Whatever brotherhood may be a sham, let the brotherhood of believers be the most real thing beneath the stars.

It would be greatly to your gain if you never again indulged a shred of hope in your own works, and were forced to accept the grace of God.

Darkness never begets light, filth never creates purity, hell never yields heaven, and depravity never produces grace.

It has sometimes happened that the illustrious deed of one man has served to elevate a class or even a nation into honor.

I believe that within a century it will be found impossible to make men believe that educated men were ever so degraded as to accept the philosophy of the present hour.

Do what you do right thoroughly, pray over it heartily, and leave the result to God.

Works done out of love to Christ, and love to saints, and love to the poor, and love to lost sinners are good works.

In Jesus we do not see humanized Godhead, nor deified manhood; but he is distinctly God and distinctly man, yet both of these are in one person, and must neither be confounded nor severed.

If your conscience gives way for the sake of your own gain or pleasure, the world will think that it is a sham, and they will not be far from the mark.

We are in a special degree God's workmanship, created to this end, that we may produce good works, and we are fitted to that end as much as a bird is fitted to fly or a worm is fitted for its purposes in the earth.

Well may we be called brethren, for we are redeemed by one blood; we are partakers of the same life; we feed upon the same heavenly food; we are united to the same living head; we seek the same ends; we love the same Father; we are heirs of the same promises, and we shall dwell forever together in the same heaven.

Out of evil comes good, through the great goodness of God.

The life of Jesus Christ is great throughout.

You cannot be saved *in* your sins; you are to be saved *from* your sins.

Those who prefer philosophy to Christ never knew Him.

We remember much that we ought to forget, and we forget much that we ought to remember.

I count no man so loathsome that God may not look upon him in love.

By faith children become little disciples, and by faith they go on to become more proficient.

Singing is the language of joy, the special vehicle of praise, the chosen speech of heaven.

Since sin was laid on Jesus, God's justice cannot lay it upon the believing sinner. The Lord will never punish twice the same offense.

There may be, there is, grace in other men, but not as it is in Christ; they have it as water flowing through a pipe, but He has it as water in its fountain and source.

Many good people there are who have religious crazes! They do nothing, but they have wonderful plans for doing everything in a jiffy.

Full often the most advantageous place for our manhood is that which is surrounded with splendid difficulties.

It is well to have Christ's portrait hung up in every chamber of your soul; I do not say of your house—that might lead to idolatry; but in every chamber of your mind and heart.

Those who preach the cross of our Lord Jesus are the terror of modern thinkers. In their heart of hearts they dread the preaching of the old-fashioned Gospel, and they hate what they dread.

Those who follow after falsehood have a secret monitor within which tells them that theirs is a weak course, and that truth must and will prevail over them. Let them alone; the beating of their own hearts will scare them.

I have heard a great deal about evolution and development, but I am afraid that if any one of us were to be developed to our utmost, apart from the grace of God, we should come out worse than before the development began.

We are not free from the worldliness which puts self first and God nowhere, else our various enterprises would be more abundantly supplied with the silver and the gold which are the Lord's, but which even professing Christians reserve for themselves.

The less we do when we go mad the better for everybody, and the less we go mad the better for ourselves.

Love is a master force, and he that feels its power will hate all evil.

There is such a thing as spoiling what you would do by making so great a fuss before you do it.

The Lord Jesus deserved to be served at the best rate and at the highest cost.

The Church is injured in her efforts for the conversion of the world by the inconsistencies of certain of her members.

Let us be silent before the Lord and judge His ways no longer, for in this judgment there is no benefit to ourselves or others.

The existence of God and the immortality of the soul lie at the basis of Old Testament teaching.

We have seen very, very, very great little people, and very, very little great people who have given themselves mighty airs; but we have never seen any good come of their greatness.

When a man is no longer afraid, but is prepared to welcome whatever comes, because he sees in it the appointment of a loving Father, why, then he is in a happy state.

A wise man will go to work in a sensible way, and will so give his money to the poor that he will be lending it to the Lord. No security can be better and no interest can be surer. The bank is open at all hours. It is the best savings bank in the nation.

The beginning of a clear sense of our own weakness is often the beginning of the display of the power of God.

In opening a new business sanctify the venture with the supplications of godly friends, and in all fresh enterprises be guided of the Lord.

Happy are we if we can while yet we live be coworkers together with Him, that when He cometh to His Kingdom we may be partakers of His glory.

To know the truth and feel its power, and manifest its influence in your life, is the proof that you have grappled it to your soul as with hooks of steel.

I am unable to frame an excuse for profane language; it is needless, willful wickedness. Men talk so as to horrify us; they chill our blood with fear lest God should take them at their word, and all for nothing at all.

Calm resignation does not come all at once; often long years of physical pain, or mental depression, or disappointment in business, or multiplied bereavements are needed to bring the soul into full submission to the will of the Lord.

Promising men are not great favorites if they are not performing men.

They that serve God shall not have to complain of His deserting them.

However good a man may be, he will not escape trial in the flesh.

Men dream, and then assert that their visions are truth.

The authority of Jesus stands to us in the stead of reasoning.

The world is a veritable Dead Sea upon a gigantic scale.

Faith has brought us into the possession of an indefeasible salvation.

The joy of religion lies in a hearty faith in it.

It is foolish to try to live on past experience; it is a very dangerous if not a fatal habit.

Idle professor, if you would be diligent in serving your Lord life would be music to you.

The young convert is an emigrant from the world, and has become, for Christ's sake, an alien.

We incline to attach undue importance to matters which are proper and useful in their places, but which are by no means essential to salvation.

Those who seek after the novelties of *this conceited century* seek to push their Lord from His place that a philosopher may fill His throne.

If you ever allow yourself to be pleased by those who speak well of you, to that extent will you be capable of being grieved by those who speak ill of you.

God sees everything as *now*. Nothing is past, nothing is future to Him. He sees things that are not as though they were, and the things that shall be as though they had been.

The powers of darkness are not so strong as they seem to be. The subtlest infidels and heretics are only men. What is more, they are bad men; and bad men at bottom are weak men.

Whenever you find sickness in a house or death in a darkened chamber, seize the opportunity to speak for your Lord. Your voice for truth will be likely to be heard, for God Himself is speaking and men must hear Him whether they will or no.

Wisdom in a poor man is like a diamond set in lead, for none but good judges can discover its value.

Lazy fellows ruin their trade and then say that bad trade ruined them.

He that is out of order with God may well be out of order with himself.

Those who dwell outside the palace of love know nothing about our secret ecstasies and raptures.

The more God blesses you, the less you shall see of any adequate reason in yourself why you should be blest.

The microscope reveals a world of marvels quite as surprising as that which is brought before us by the telescope.

The moment the Lord Jesus Christ saves a soul He gives that soul strength for its appointed service.

If there were no hereafter, the immediate peace and joy of trusting my God are an overflowing reward.

Always have something in hand that is greater than your present capacity. Grow up to it, and when you have grown up to it, grow more.

So you may be a Christian and be weak, timorous, and sad, but this is not desirable; it is better to be a happy, holy, vigorous, useful Christian.

We think we can do what we are not called to, and if by chance the thing falls to our lot we do worse than those we blamed.

We want a conversion which shall make us run in *parallel lines with the God* who has revealed Himself by His prophets and apostles and by His ever-to-be-adored Son.

Some people can do anything that they are allowed to do, but waste their energies in lamenting that they are not called on to do other people's work.

He who can touch the secret springs of the heart, apart from circumstances and conditions, has often made a man glad when he has been racked with pain, or when he has been in the depths of poverty, or when he has been suffering at the demoniacal hands of inquisitors.

To you is given not gold, nor silver, nor precious stones to fashion, but immortal spirits that shall glorify Christ on earth and in heaven.

The Gospel is not sent to men to gratify their curiosity by letting them see how other people get to heaven. Christ did not come to amuse us, but to redeem us.

The enemy can use humility for his purpose as well as pride. Whether he makes us think too much or too little of our work, it is all the same to him, so long as he can get us off from it.

He that lavished money when he had it feels the want of it all the more when it is gone.

I think you will find that tried saints are the most biblical saints.

Everything seems lost, and yet as long as a man can look to God nothing is lost.

Jesus founded His empire upon love and His own self-sacrifice is the corner-stone of that imperial fabric.

I have never known more blissful seasons than those which my Lord vouchsafed me when I was abused by men and had to fight a weary battle.

The Godly must die, even as others. Though our life be perfectly consecrated, yet it cannot forever be continued in this world.

The acquisition of property often decreases a man rather than adds to him. Have you not seen a man become visibly smaller as his riches grew greater?

The spirit of the true man answers to this: He is always willing to set in order the court of conscience, and makes solemn trial of his heart and life.

A hard-working young man with his wits about him will make money where others do nothing but lose it.

A thousand instances prove that only by endurance can names be graven in the brass of history. To make a man a man, to bring his manhood forward, and to make other men see it, there must be endurance.

Be first a man of God, after that a banker, or a merchant, or a workingman. Then the secondary character would rise in excellence and nobility.

I know your sorrows make an excursion to the grave to look there for the deceased ones. You want to lift that coffin-lid and to unwrap the shroud. Oh, do not so, do not so! He is not here; the real man has gone. He may be dead to you for awhile, but he lives unto God. Yes, the dead one liveth, he liveth unto God.

I expect that if you go into the business of mending yourself you will be like the man who had an old gun and took it to the gunsmith, and the gunsmith said, "Well, this would make a very good gun if it had a new stock and a new lock and a new barrel." So you would make a very good man by mending if you had a new heart and a new life, and were made new all over, so that there was not a bit of the old stuff left. It will be easier, a great deal, depend upon it, even for God to make you new than to mend you. What is wanted is that you should be made a new creature in Christ Jesus.

Before you begin a thing make sure it is the right thing to do; ask Mr. Conscience about it. Do not try to do what is impossible; ask Common Sense.

Deep sincerity breeds in a man a blessed indifference to the judgments of men.

Adversity is the richest field in all the farm of life.

Love the soul of every man with all the intensity of thy being.

To tell out the heart to a patient listener is a great relief to a burdened spirit, and the heart must do it in its own way.

Many people would like to *go to heaven by an underground railway;* secrecy suits them.

The religion of Jesus is unselfish; it enlists a man as a crusader against everything that is unrighteous.

Those who believe in Jesus may be called fools to-day, but men will think otherwise when they see them shine forth as the sun in the Father's kingdom.

We are knights of the Red Cross, and our bloodless battles are against all things that degrade our fellow-men, whether they be causes social, political, or religious.

God has been very merciful to some of us in never letting money come rolling in upon us, for most men are carried off their legs if they meet with a great wave of fortune. Many of us would have been bigger sinners if we had been trusted with larger purses.

Religion must not be like a fine piece of mediæval armor, to be hung upon the wall, or only worn on state occasions. No; it is a garment for the house, the shop, the bank.

To say there is a God is not much. It is the same as to say there is a bank; but there may be a bank, and you may be miserably poor. There certainly is a God, but that God may be no source of comfort to you. The joy of the whole thing lies in that word "my." *My* God will hear me.

Yonder young woman knows that according to God's word she must not marry that young man, for she would be unequally yoked together with an unbeliever. Now, she was quite willing to be baptized, and she is heartily willing to give her money to the Lord, and in fact to do anything except that one act of self-denial, which would require her to cease from a fond friendship. Yet, my friend, I do not know what sorrow you will make for yourself if you really break that salutary rule. I have seen many instances of mixed marriages, but I have had to mourn over nearly all of them as the cause of untold wretchedness.

He who talks forever about himself has a foolish subject, and is likely to worry and weary all around him.

True religion is diffusive and extensive in its operations.

The indifference to Scripture is the great curse of the Church at this hour.

The hand of faith is against all evil, and all evil is against faith.

Men of the world teach us the value of joyous song. How readily the anchor rises when the sailors unite in cheery cries.

Our temptations are no inventions of nervousness nor hobgoblins of dreamy fear.

As we would desire to receive sympathy and help in our hour of need, let us render it freely to those who are now enduring trial.

An old man with his bones filled with the sin of his youth is a dreadful sight to look upon; he is a curse to others and a burden to himself.

Much of history is happily covered with a veil, so that its secret griefs do not become open miseries, else were the world too wretched for a tender heart to live in it.

Every generous heart delights to think that "the poor have the gospel preached unto them."

Ask Him to keep you in check, that you may not be working mischief in your haste which you will have to repent of in your leisure.

History must repeat itself so long as we have the same human nature to deal with, the same sins to ensnare mankind, the same truth to be trifled with, and the same devil to stir men up to the same mischief.

True we shall pass through that river which is named Death; but it is a misnomer; like the Jordan when Isreal passed into Canaan, the Lord hath rebuked it, and it is dried up. We shall pass through the valley of the shadow of death, and that is all; and thus we shall reach a higher stage of being, in which we shall be "forever with the Lord."

John Ploughman feels a cold sweat at the thought of getting into the hands of lawyers. He does not mind going to Jericho, but he dreads the gentlemen on the road, for they seldom leave a feather upon any goose which they pick up. However, if men will fight they must not blame the lawyers; if law were cheaper, quarrelsome people would have more of it, and quite as much would be spent in the long run. Sometimes, however, we get dragged into court willy nilly, and then one had need be wise as a serpent and harmless as a dove. Happy is he who finds an honest lawyer and does not try to be his own client.

Before a man cracks a joke he should consider how he would like it himself, for many who give rough blows have very thin skins. Give only what you would be willing to take.

There is grace for the man who quits his sin, but there is tribulation and wrath upon every man who doeth evil.

Think also how much the world is injured by Christians who are not Christians.

Nothing in the Gospel excuses sin; nothing in it affords toleration for lust or anger, or dishonesty or falsehood.

Thine open confession of Him in His own appointed way shall bring thee a fuller realization of salvation.

Health is far more to be prized than wealth or honor or learning.

The resurrection of Christ is the world's great hope concerning those that are asleep.

No man talks of living without sin till he is taken in the net of self-deception.

A world of sorrow comes through people not having made their wills. Have everything in order.

The smile of a mother's face has enticed many into the right path, and the fear of bringing a tear into her eye has called off many a man from evil ways. The boy may have a heart of iron, but his mother can hold him like a magnet.

If bodily filthiness is horrible to us, what must the filthiness of sin be to the pure and holy God.

The history of grace begins earlier and goes on later, but in its middle point stands the cross. Of two eternities this is the hinge; of past decrees and future glories this is the pivot.

Blessed above all other beings are those who have Jehovah to be their God and who are themselves the Lord's choice and care and delight.

We dare say it very reverently, that we have a claim upon God when we are His servants. Of course, that claim is only such as He allows, and it is founded alone on grace; but still it is a strong plea with our gracious Master.

It is a very curious thing that some of God's servants do draw a very great deal of consolation from comparatively trivial things. We are all the creatures of sentiment as well as of reason, and hence we are often strongly affected by little things. But what a pity it is that we should need such little bits of things to cheer us up, when we have matters of far surer import to make us glad!

Let us pray for those who never pray for themselves: God's power can do for them what is far beyond our power.

Encouragement is due to young converts.

Even our apparent ills have been real blessings.

Without a spiritual motive the best work is dead.

Often the greatest of moral acts are done in secret.

Some persons when they are angry will say things that never ought to be repeated, or even said for the first time.

It is an instinct of the new life to rejoice in the salvation of souls.

Jesus must have the pre-eminence among men, since he is in person and character pre-eminent.

Buckle on your harness to war against your sins, for He will give you power to overcome them.

If a fellow takes the trouble to flatter he expects to be paid for it, and he calculates that he will get his wages out of the soft brains of those he tickles.

If we fetch our supplies from Him, if we move only at His bidding, if we intensely love Him, we shall be a people to be envied by all who know us.

Demons that gather about our last hour shall flee away as bats fly out of a cavern scared by a torch; they shall flee when they hear the voice, "Behold, he prayeth."

It is a good thing to be under the sound of the Word of God. Even if the very lowest motive should induce persons to come to hear the Gospel, it is nevertheless a good thing that they should come.

"This same Jesus shall so come in like manner. He went up as a matter of fact; not in poetic figure and spiritual symbol, but as a matter of fact—"This same Jesus" literally went up. "This same Jesus" *will literally come again.* He will descend in clouds even as He went up in clouds.

I shall forever respect the memory of a humble servant in the school wherein I was usher at Newmarket—an old woman, who talked with me concerning the things of the kingdom, and taught me the way of the Lord more perfectly. She knew the doctrines of grace better than many a doctor of divinity, and she held them with the tenacious grasp of one who found her life in them. It was my great privilege to help her in her old age, and but a little while ago she passed away to heaven. Many things did I learn of her which to-day I delight to preach.

They say a brain is worth little if you have not a tongue; but what is a tongue worth without a brain?

Begin each day by giving the dew of the morning to communion with heaven.

Let every thief know that the dying thief entered heaven by faith in Jesus.

If the Lord Jesus Christ were to come to-day I should like Him to find me at my studying, praying, or preaching.

If you hunt the butterfly of wealth too eagerly you may spoil it by the stroke with which you secure it.

He has gained more than he has lost, even though he has lost everything, if he has gained contentment, conformity to the will of God, a deep experience, and a surer hope.

It is not wisdom which leads teachers to become obscure; if they teach at all they should adapt themselves to the disciple's capacity.

When men believe in lawyers and money-lenders (whether Jews or Gentiles), and borrow money, and speculate, and think themselves lucky fellows, they are shamefully *ignorant.*

There never was a serener mind than that of Jesus Christ our Lord.

Our way is up the river; we have to stem the current and struggle against a flood which would readily bear us to destruction.

Companions for apostles are only to be produced in the school of Holy Scripture. Those who have communed with Moses and David and the prophets are fit to associate with an apostle.

There dwells upon this earth a mysterious Being, whose office is to renew the fallen and restore the wandering. We cannot see Him, or hear Him, yet He dwells in some of us as Lord of our nature. His chosen residence is a broken heart and a contrite spirit.

Draw not the beloved bodies to the cemetery with dreary pomp and with black horses, but cover the coffin with sweet flowers and drape the horses with emblems of hope. It is the better birthday of the saint, yea, his truer wedding-day. Is it sad to have done with sadness? Is it sorrowful to part with sorrow?

I have sometimes thought to myself that it were better if there were no water baptism, seeing that it has become the nest of so much superstition; and the Lord's Supper, with all its blessed uses, has been so abused that one is apt to think that without outward ordinances there might be more spiritual religion; but the Lord intends that the materialism of man and of creation shall be uplifted, and that the body shall be raised incorruptible, and therefore has He given seals which touch the outward and material.

Poor men will always be poor if they think they must be.

Prayer will do anything—will do everything.

Whatsoever the Lord doeth is full of wisdom, and the wise will search into it.

There is now no spot on earth where God dwells in preference to another.

Serve the Lord in some way or other; serve Him always; serve Him intensely; serve Him more and more.

The Gospel offers you no opportunity of going on in sin and escaping without punishment.

The faith that saves is not always full-grown; there is room for us to believe more, and to expect more, of our blessed Lord.

Certain neighbors of mine laugh at me for being a tee-totaller, and I might well laugh at them for being drunken, only I feel more inclined to cry that they should be such fools.

It will be an awful thing for the man who used profane imprecations to find out at last that his prayers were heard, and that they will be answered.

Alas! that men should sin away their souls so lightly, as if self-destruction were some merry game that they were playing at, whereas it is a heaping up unto themselves wrath against the day of wrath.

Faith is the queen bee. You may get temperance, love, hope, and all those other bees into the hive; but the main thing is to get simple faith in Christ, and all the rest will come afterward.

Could we lift the tops of the houses, could we exhibit the skeletons hidden in closets, could we take away the curtains from human breasts, what sorrows we should see; and the mass of those sorrows—not the whole of them, but the mass—would be found to come from sin.

I often see upon a sunny wall a chrysalis, and when I go to take it down I find that the summer's sun has shone upon it and the insect has developed, and left nothing but an empty case behind. How often in the pew we find the chrysalis of a man, but where is the man himself? Wait till to-morrow morning, and see him in his shop; there is the man; or, to follow up the figure, there is the butterfly with all its wings. Wait till you find our friend engaged in secular employment to his own advantage, and then you will see what he is made of; but in the work of the Lord he is not worth his salt.

Better kind words to the living than fine speeches over the grave.

Grace does not run in the blood, but we generally find that the Timothies have mothers of a godly sort.

A mocking word cuts worse than a scythe, and the wound is harder to heal. A blow is much sooner forgotten than a jeer.

Waste is of Satan, not of God.

Some men are blinded by their worldly business, and could not see heaven itself if the windows were open over their heads.

If ever you live to want what you once wasted, it will fill you with woe enough to last you to your grave.

If you want to be secure never stand as security for any living man, woman, child, youth, maiden, cousin, brother, uncle, or mother-in-law.

Begin early to teach, for children begin early to sin. Catch them young and you may hope to keep them.

Often debt is the worst kind of poverty, because it breeds deceit. Men do not like to face their circumstances, and so they turn their backs on the truth.

If a man cannot pay his debts he must not think of giving, for he has nothing of his own, and it is thieving to give away other people's property.

There is a text, a very short one, which I would like often to preach from, in reference to those who are newly saved, and I would invite you continually to be practicing it: that text is, "Encourage him."

Whenever there is a holy deed to be done, our mathematical-minded unbelievers are prompt with their estimates of cost and their prudent forecastings of grave deficiencies. We are great at calculations when we are little at believing.

To doubt is natural to fallen men, for we have within us an evil heart of unbelief. It is abominably wicked, I grant you; but still it is natural, because of the downward tendency of our depraved hearts.

I heard a brother in a prayer-meeting say, "The Lord hath done great things for us, whereof we *desire to be* glad;" and I wanted to jump down that man's throat and pull that passage back again and put it into its natural shape.

In our utterances there has been faith mixed with unbelief, love defaced with a want of submission, gratitude combined with distrust, humility flavored with self-conceit, courage undermined with cowardice, fervor mingled with indifference.

He who never owns that he is wrong will never get right.

Little things please little minds and nasty things please dirty minds.

Wit should be a shield for defense and not a sword for offense.

There is not one among us who has lived a day without sin.

Christ and a crust is riches, but a broken character is the worst of bankruptcy.

Beware of trusting all your secrets with anybody but your wife.

It is wise to marry when we can marry wisely, and then the sooner the better.

He that earns an estate will keep it better than he that inherits it.

Perseverance is the main thing in life. To hold on and hold out to the end is the chief matter.

Everybody who does not get on lays it all on competition.

A man never listens to reason when he has made up his mind to act unreasonably.

Those who despise their neighbors come to be despised themselves.

People don't think much of a man's piety when his promises are like pie-crust, made to be broken.

Everybody should know what most concerns him and makes him most useful.

Stick to your calling, plod on, and be content; for, make sure, if you can *undergo* you shall *overcome*.

Use each thing and each man according to common-sense and you will be uncommonly sensible.

A boy can be driven to learn till he loses half his wits; forced fruits have little flavor; a man at five is a fool at fifteen.

Never mind the coat, give me the man; shells are nothing, the kernel is everything.

There must be something very much amiss about a man who is not missed when he dies.

Of all dust the worst for the eyes is gold dust. A bribe blinds the judgment, and riches darken the mind.

We are all at school, and our great Teacher writes many a bright lesson on the black-board of affliction.

If you are going to be a champion of reformation, first be yourself reformed.

It is in the Lord's word that the hope of His people finds support.

The most abominable beings out of hell are Christians without Christianity; and there are plenty of them.

The Lord Jesus always owns a faith which comes toward him, however lame it may be.

To draw Him nearer to me, and myself nearer to Him, is the innermost longing of my soul.

Let all the necessities of men impel you, compel you, constrain you to be blessing them.

The world is always looking to the Church, not so much to hear her teachings as to see her doings.

He has an opportunity for distinguishing himself who is placed amid temptations and perils.

I cannot imagine an occasion for glorifying God equal to the fact that man has sinned, since God has given Christ to die for sinners.

Happy is the man who is happy in his wife. Let him love her as he loves himself, and a little better, for she is his better half.

I would not have a converted person wait a week before trying to do something for Jesus. Run as soon as you find your feet.

He will certainly come in His own person to reward His saints; and ere He comes He sees what you are doing. If this does not nerve you to tireless diligence in holy service, what can?

Instead of being discouraged because what we do is unworthy of God, and insignificant compared with what was done by others, let us gather up our strength to reform our errors and reach to higher attainments.

When old age comes on and memory fails me, that which my soul shall hold as a death grip will not be historical remembrance, classical lore, or theological learning, but what she knows by inward experience of the Lord her God.

If my Lord should say to me, "From this hour I will always answer your prayer just as you pray it," the first petition I would offer would be, "*Lord, do nothing of the sort.*" Because that would be putting the responsibility of my life upon myself, instead of allowing it to remain upon God.

Those who are quick to promise are generally slow to perform.

Gladness is the privilege of saints.

Real prayer cannot come from men whose characters are contrary to the mind of God.

If you would have Christ for a Saviour you must also take Him for a King.

A fool soon makes up his mind, because there is so very little of it; but a wise man waits and considers.

Those saints who have been in glory now these thousands of years cannot be more blessed than the latest arrivals.

The right thing is to feel that the more God loves you the more you love Him; the more He does for you the more will you do for Him.

The secret sustenance of the soul by God is very precious. It is not observed of men, but therein the saints are made to magnify their God.

It is better to be a good housewife, or nurse, or domestic servant than to be a powerless preacher or a graceless talker.

There are many in this world who ignore sorrow, who pass by grief, who are deaf to lamentation and blind to distress.

Children of prayer will grow up to be children of praise; mothers who have wept before God for their sons will one day sing a new song over them.

The points in which there is a weakness in your natural constitution and in which you have made failures are the points at which you must set a double guard.

Just now the great thing is to see how you and I can get evil out of the world, and how we can lift up the fallen and restore those who have gone astray.

He whose faith stands upon the concensus of popular opinion has placed his feet upon the sand, but he who has read his Bible and has been taught of the Spirit of God what truth is will hold to it, come what may.

Apart from the glories of heaven I would wish to live trusting in my God and resting in Him for this present life, since I need his present aid for every day as truly as I shall need it at the last day.

London is worse than a wilderness to many; a man may lay himself down and die in these streets and nobody will care for him. The millions will pass him by, not for want of kindness, but from want of thought. There is no such horrible wilderness as a wilderness of men.

They are most apt to speak ill of others who do most ill themselves.

Many a woman is destroyed by her clothes.

Many a man is destroyed by his eating.

London is *a simmering caldron of vice* and crime.

Our sicknesses are of the Lord's appointing.

When man acts according to God's order he lives.

Of how small account is the judgment of men.

Ignorance of spelling books is very bad, but ignorance of hard work is worse.

Ah, friend, if the grace of God by trial shall work in you the quiet patience which never grows angry and never ceases to love, you may have lost a trifle of comfort, but you have gained a solid weight of character.

He that soweth the seed of heresy and evil doctrine entails upon succeeding generations an evil and a plague, and his very name shall rot; but he that soweth the good seed shall be the father of ten thousand successive harvests.

If we are to live, let us live to noble purpose. It would be a great pity to lose a single year, much less a long life. If you are going to live a hundred years, begin them with God.

We are looking forward to His second advent for the uplifting of the Church to a higher platform than that upon which it now stands. Then shall the militant become triumphant, and the laboring become exultant.

There is one person who plagues you; if you could only get away from him, you would be content; but that person happens to be yourself, and there appears to be no rest for you, either in company or in solitude.

Though it may seem a very small thing to grieve a pious child or to vex a poor, godly woman, God does not think it so. He remembers jests and scoffs leveled at His little ones, and He bids those who indulge in them to take heed.

✓Even the thoughtless or trifling repetition of the name of the Lord involves great sin, for thus a man taketh the sacred name in vain; yet men trifle with that name in common conversation, and that with fearful frequency.

Studying the lives of eminent men, we come to this conclusion, that on the whole it is good for a man to bear the yoke; good for a man to breast the billows; good for a man to pass through fire and through water, and so to learn sublime lessons.

All the wit in the world is not in one head, and therefore the wisest man living is not bound to look after all his neighbors' matters.

Much of what is called prayer is the husk, and not the kernel, of prayer.

Each hour of sin brings its hardness and its difficulty of change.

The desire of unholy gain is called filthy lucre, because it leads men to do dirty deeds which else they would not think of.

God's children always play the fool when they play the judge; they are never in order when they act as if they were the head of the family of grace.

Some of us may spend our next Sabbath with the angels. Let us rejoice and be glad at the bare thought of it.

When you feel most unfit to resort to God you may still go to Him, for He is your fitness and your physician.

No signs can be more alarming than the growing infidelity and worldliness which I see among those who call themselves Christians.

If a man calls himself my friend and leaves the ways of God, then his way and mine are different; he who is no friend to the good cause is no friend of mine.

The Lord likes His servants to have such an experience that their testimony shall have *a man at the back of it.* He would have their lives sustain and explain their testimonies.

I might curse myself seven times deep by a prayer within the next seven minutes, if there were no safeguards and limits to the promise of prayer being answered.

Who are the people that give up holy practice? Why, the people that are not dwelling in the power of the Holy Ghost, and are not full of the life of God.

Consciences used to work up and down, yes or no; but now they have an eccentric action, altogether indescribable. A man serves the devil nowadays and gets the devil's pay, and all the while talks of serving God.

In grace you can be under bonds, yet not in bondage. I am in the bonds of wedlock, but I feel no bondage; on the contrary, it is a joy to be so bound. The bond of grace is a marriage bond, uniting us to Him whom we love above all, even the altogether lovely Bridegroom of our souls.

Our Lord and Saviour came when time was full and like a harvest ready for His reaping, and *so will He come again when once more the age is ripe* and ready for His presence.

I would sooner be a cat on hot bricks or a toad under a harrow than let my own children be my masters.

Rest you assured that God will care for you if you make His service your delight.

The whole course of the Lord's dealing is calculated to inspire confidence.

The mass of us cannot go abroad as missionaries, but we can all be messengers for Christ in our own city.

Nothing hardens like the Gospel when it is long trifled with. To lie asoak in the truth without receiving it into the heart is sure destruction.

Do what the Lord bids you, when He bids you, where He bids you, as He bids you, as long as He bids you, and do it at once.

When you relieve the wants of a man in health you may possibly assist him in his vices, but in helping the sick poor you can do no wrong,

If you have been on the borders of the grave and the Gospel has given you joy and gladness, then you know how true it is. Experimental knowledge is the best and surest.

God seems to talk to me in every primrose and daisy, to smile upon me from every star, to whisper to me in every breath of morning air, and to call aloud to me in every storm.

I cannot convey to you a sense of the joy of a face uplifted unto God. You must feel it for yourselves, by lifting up your own faces.

Let us build our God a house of praises; let us lay the deep foundations in love, set up the pillars with gratitude, and roof in the whole with joyous hallelujahs.

There are so many gates to the grave. We can die anywhere, at any time, by any means. Not alone abroad are we in danger, but at home in security we are still in peril.

We dare not say that we have kept the ten commands from our youth up; on the contrary, we are compelled by our consciences to confess that in spirit and in heart, if not in act, we have continually broken the law of God.

If you professing Christian people are as greedy and hard as other people in your dealings with the world, and if in your families you are as quarrelsome and untruthful as the ungodly, God cannot come to your tabernacles.

Whatever men in their folly may talk as to neglecting the outward means and sitting still and doing nothing because God will do his own work, we hear nothing of the kind from Jesus. Therefore, despise not means, and at the same time do not rest in them.

He who will not go to bed till he pleases everybody will have to sit up a great many nights.

The Lord will fulfill His word thoroughly.

Loving-kindness underlies and overlays His wrath.

The conquering weapon of the Christian is love.

A man of God is not prepared to enjoy success till he has tasted defeat.

Faith is the fighting principle and the conquering principle. By faith God is greatly glorified, and hence by faith Satan is greatly annoyed.

Very early in life some are brought to Jesus with little terror or distress of mind. Let them be very grateful for it.

It is a solemn thing to have God so near, but the joy is equal to the solemnity.

Blessed shall that man be who has no answer to give to God's call but just "Here am I."

We should, in all probability, see a much more rapid growth in grace among our young converts if they were better nursed and watched over. Amen!

It is a sin to put people where they are likely to sin. If you believe the old saying, that when you set a beggar on horseback he will ride to the devil, don't let him have a horse of yours.

Christ's discipleship is always practical; it is of the heart and of the hand as well as of the head.

Your conviction that you are clean before God will give you confidence in telling out to others the story of the cross.

At home one might not have all the skill of the hospital at command, but one would be sure of a certain priceless tenderness which no nurse can rival.

The man of God is pricked and torn by the briers of the age in which he travels; he is vexed and wearied with the bribery and corruption all around him.

I do not wonder that men who have tasted of the grace of God, and feel that the Lord has done great things for them, whereof they are glad, do feel like crying out for joy.

Give me the man who understands that second thoughts are not always the best, for they are apt to chill, and the best thought is that which comes from a heart fired with the love of Christ; but that same characteristic, if not kept in proper order by the Spirit of God, may lead you into a world of mischief.

Religious deceivers are the worst of vermin.

Now is the time of battle, but the second advent shall bring both victory and rest.

To judge according to outward circumstances has been the tendency of men in all times.

The Lord knows the street and He knows the house where the sinner lives who is to be blessed by Him.

Remember that your own thoughts of what God is are far from being correct unless they are drawn from His own revelation.

Grace delights in dealing with great and glaring sin and putting away the crying crimes of great offenders.

Those who are most afflicted in this life may have the highest glory in the life to come.

Might not the Lord stand in a prayer-meeting and hear a dozen of us talk our piece and never say, "Behold, he prayeth?"

There is an adaptation in the Bible for human beings of all ages, and therefore it has a fitness for children.

When a true child of God is in trouble it is wonderful how dear the Bible becomes to him—ay, the very words of it.

When a boy is rebellious, conquer him, and do it well the first time, that there may be no need to do it again. A child's first lesson should be obedience, and after that you may teach it what you please.

Happy is the man who has been enabled to endure; he rises from the deeps of woe like a pearl-finder from the sea, rich beyond comparison.

God takes the meaning of our groans and tears, and when we fail to express ourselves suitably in words He reads our hearts and accepts our secret meanings.

I have distinctly seen a man become "the architect of his own fortune" and the destroyer of himself. He has built up a palatial estate upon the ruins of his own manhood.

There are no loose threads in the providence of God, no stitches are dropped, no events are left to chance. *The great clock of the universe* keeps good time, and the whole machinery of Providence moves with unerring punctuality.

I think we have read enough of the history of God's dealings with His people to understand that this is the way of Him—that if He ever is absent from His people it is not in their time of direst need, and if ever He does reveal Himself to them as He does not unto the world it is when they are bereaved of all outward consolation and for His sake are made to bear tribulation.

There are fools enough in the world, and there can be no need that Christian men should swell the number.

Hell, however painted, is never so terrible a thing as the death which fills it.

This sacred book is infallible, but not our thoughts.

We are all odd in some way or other.

Obedience is the best of worship.

Our zeal for God ought to be as fresh as if we had just begun to delight in Him.

One of the surest evidences of a living faith is prayer.

Jesus has not come into the world to make sin less terrible.

If our faith is to grow exceedingly we must maintain constant intercourse with God.

When a man speaks so that you cannot understand him, the usual reason is that he does not understand himself.

The confession of sin, the longing for mercy, the groaning for grace—these are the soul and spirit of prayer.

It is grand when the wife knows her place and keeps it, and they both pull together in everything. Then she is a helpmeet indeed and makes the house a home.

I reckon that those prayers which cannot be expressed in language are often the most deep and fervent.

Persistence in known sin, and especially indulgence in enmity and hatred, are so destructive to prayer that till we are free from them we do not pray.

If you feel quite content with your own prayers, permit me to suggest that you do not pray, for few who pray aright are ever content with their own petitions.

Those who dream themselves to belong to *the Good-enough family* will find themselves bad enough, and the Too-goods will find themselves shut out of heaven.

You that are the people of God, you may sometimes in your willfulness wish that you could get away from the all-searching eye; but if you could do so it would be hell to you.

The devil never reckons a man to be lost so long as he has a good mother alive.

If we begin, continue, and end with God, our way will be strewn with blessings.

Plunge yourself into your work with whole-hearted devotion, and you shall yet discover some hidden jewel which shall adorn Immanuel's diadem.

Young men have flung away all hope of salvation in order that they might be thought to be men of culture; they have abjured faith in order to be esteemed "free-thinkers" by those whose opinions were not worth a pin's head. I charge you, dear friend, if you are beginning at all to be a slave of other people, break these wretched and degrading bonds.

That which a man does when he thinks that he is entirely by himself is the best revelation of the man.

You are not half as happy as you might be, because you do not study the Book, wherein, as in a glass, you may see the face of Jehovah your God.

If you stand half a mile off from a man and throw the Gospel at him you will miss him, but if you go close to him and lay hold upon him, giving him a hearty grip of the hand, and show that you have an affection for him, you will, by God's blessing, lead him in the right way.

You can never pray an inch beyond the tether of the promise with any assurance of being heard. For my own part, I always feel on sure ground with God when I can quote His own words.

Sensible men don't marry a wardrobe or a bonnet-box; they want a woman of sense, and women of that kind always dress sensibly and not gaudily.

Do not bury a man before he is dead; hope that so long as a sinner lives he may yet live unto God. Be hopeful that He who placed this sinner in your way and you in the sinner's way has designs of love which are about to be accomplished.

True religion is always personal, but it becomes wonderfully so when a man is specially arrested by sovereign grace; for then he adores as if he were the only man in the universe, and beholds God as if no other eye throughout all the ages had ever beheld him.

He who thinks it easy to bring up a family never had one of his own.

Babes receive impressions long before we are aware of the fact. During the first months of a child's life it learns more than we imagine.

What numbers of professors I have known who go into one place of worship and hear one form of doctrine and apparently approve it because the preacher is "a clever man!" They hear an opposite teaching, and they are equally at home, because again it is "a clever man!" They join with a church, and you ask them, "Do you agree with the views of that community?" They neither know nor care what those views may be; one doctrine is as good as another to them. Their spiritual appetite can enjoy soap as well as butter; they can digest bricks as well as bread. These religious ostriches have a marvelous power of swallowing everything; they have no spiritual discernment, no appreciation of truth. They follow any "clever" person, and in this prove that they are not the sheep of our Lord's pasture.

The best piece of furniture *I have ever had in my house* is the cross of affliction.

Life is long to look forward to; but I appeal to every aged person whether it is not very short to look back upon.

Without a scriptural training a convert has no grit, no backbone, and no soul in him.

If you want power in prayer you must have purity in life.

To day *the world's one and only remedy* is the cross.

It is one thing to believe there is a God, but it is quite another thing to know it by coming into personal contact with Him.

Happy are they among women who see their sons and their daughters walking in the truth.

The system of salvation by atonement is calculated to produce truthful men.

If thou hast a faith which looks to ceremonies, creeds, prayers, and feelings it will fail thee when most thou needest help.

If wealth and righteousness run counter to each other, let the gold perish, but hold thou fast to righteousness.

Many a man has thrown his soul away for a little honor, or for the transient satisfaction of success in trifles.

We must preach the coming of the Lord, and preach it somewhat more than we have done, because it is the driving power of the Gospel.

Contemplation of Christ Himself may be so carried out as to lead you away from Christ; the recluse meditates on Jesus, but he is as unlike the busy, self-denying Jesus as well can be.

God can work by any means. He can never be short of instruments. For his battles he can find weapons on the hearth, weapons in the kneading-trough, weapons in the poor man's basket.

Those Psalms are marvelous. *David seems to have lived for us all;* he was not so much one man as all men in one. Somewhere or other, the great circle of his experience touches yours and mine, and the Holy Ghost by David has furnished us with the best expressions which we can utter before the Lord in prayer.

Some fools are left alive to write on the monuments of those who are buried.

Many will only act as others act; they must keep in the fashion.

Every one that is born of the Spirit of God is brother to every other that is born of the same Spirit.

We have never reached the sum of our grace-given privileges till we are more at home with God than with any one else in the universe.

No man knoweth what villainy he is capable of; he only needs to be placed under certain circumstances and he will develop into a very fiend.

If you want anything done well do it yourself, with this exception—that *if you want your character defended you should always let that alone.*

It matters not to you or me what nationality He actually came from, for the most cosmopolitan of men was the Christ of God.

Too much cunning overdoes its work, and in the long run there is no craft which is so wise as simple honesty.

Can we be busy with earthly cares all the six days of the week and be ready for the holy Sabbath without a thought? I trow not.

Most kings inherit what other swords have won, but Jesus himself with His own blood hath purchased a kingdom to Himself.

The Gospel gives man a hope, and that is a grand thing for the degraded and self-condemned.

It is a great deal better to sift an affair to the bottom than it is to be always tormented by suspicion.

We meet with a certain class of men who are rather pert and forward, as the fashion of the day is in certain quarters; and then we do not think so much of *them* as they do of themselves.

Do not let us suffer our lamentations to be written in a book and our thanksgivings to be spoken to the wind. Write not your complaints in marble and your praises upon the sand.

Ask those that have had to live with converted people whether the transformation has not been marvelous. Christ makes new servants, new masters, new friends, new brothers, new sisters.

You can do a great many things with a dead man, but you cannot make him stand upright; you may try most earnestly, but a corpse cannot stand; until you put life into the body it will fall to the ground; and so if the life of God be not in you you cannot hold the truth, or maintain purity, or walk in integrity.

We have more blessings than we can count, even now.

He who prays trusts, and thus reveals the faith which saves.

You cannot call back the words which now cause you to bite your tongue with regret.

The trial of temptation of each man is distinct from that of every other.

What a sinful power imagination is, and how difficult it is to govern it.

We need trials as a test as much as we need divine truth as our food.

His was a grand life-work, but He never seemed to be confused, excited, worried, or hurried, as certain of His people are.

Get a firm confidence in God and you need not inquire what is going to happen; all must be well with you.

Sanctified trouble has a great tendency to breed *sympathy*, and sympathy is to the church as oil to machinery.

A father will not stand by to see his child abused, and the Great Father above is as tender and fond as any other father.

Manhood is a great deep. I set it not side by side with the fathomless abyss of Godhead, but I know of nothing else which surpasses it.

Inside a man's heart there is need of a thorough plowing by God's grace, for if any part of our nature is left to itself the weeds of sin smother the soul.

You, my Christian brother, cannot fall into sin without its being poison to you, as well as to anybody else; in fact, to you it is more evidently poison than to those hardened to it.

Self-denial and taking up the cross are but forms of blessedness. If we seek first the kingdom of God and His righteousness all other things shall be added to us.

Some of the purest Christians that have ever lived have had the most sickness to bear, and by that means they have been made more meet for heaven, even as the sycamore fig by being bruised becomes ripe.

It is only foolish persons who will not mention death. If you are all right with God, it can be no trouble to you to remember that as your years multiply there must be so many the fewer in which you are to abide here below.

A world where everything was easy would be a nursery for babies, but not at all a fit place for men.

Believers ought to be unutterably happy.

Time was, whenever I heard a sceptical remark, I felt wounded and somewhat shaken. I am no longer shaken by these wandering winds. There are certain things of which I am as sure as of my own existence; I have seen, tasted, and handled them, and I am past being argued out of them by those who know nothing about them.

It is appointed unto men once to die, and that appointment stands.

God will hear *us* when we hear *Him;* He will do our will when we do His will.

It is a grand thing to know what we are living for, and to live for a worthy object with the undivided energy of our being.

Every now and then we need a few drops of the oil of gladness to make the wheels of our work move pleasantly.

An alms given to the poor is good as a work of humanity, but it will be only a dead work if a desire to be seen of men is found at the bottom of it.

Prudence is wisdom, for it adapts means to ends; but anxiety is folly, for it groans and worries and accomplishes nothing.

Another part of the believer's great gain lies in the consciousness that all things are working together for his good.

You cannot ask the Lord to bless you because of any desert or merit you have, for you have no trace of any such thing, but you will be wise to plead your necessities.

When a man thinks that his place is below him he will pretty soon be below his place, and therefore a good opinion of your own calling is by no means an evil.

Remember that perdition for the orthodox will be quite as horrible as eternal ruin for the heterodox. It will be a dreadful thing to go to hell with a sound head and a rotten heart.

Do not slice pieces out of your manhood and then hope to fill up the vacancies with bank notes. He who loses manliness or godliness to gain gold is a great cheater of himself.

I believe that as a child of God grows in sanctification he deepens in humility, and as he advances to perfection he sinks in his own esteem.

Whenever the coming of our Lord shall be—and oh that it were to day, for we never wanted Him more than now!—whenever His second advent shall take place, it shall not be a dishonor to the Church, but it will be her glory to triumph with the King at her head.

What a wretched business it must be to be in dread of your own thoughts! You dare not sit alone in your chamber for half an hour and think, because if you did you would begin to think of dying, and you could not bear to think of that without a God.

Who would win must learn to bear.

It is for the truly spiritual that God reserves the choicest of His dainties.

The Scriptures do not save, but they are able to make a man wise unto salvation.

The man who truly possesses patience is the man that has been tried.

Some men are always very ready at counting the pennies which they have not got.

Undue anxiety is very common among city men, and it is not rare anywhere.

If you are too precise may the Lord set you on fire and consume your bonds of red tape!

If our life be of grace there is no room for boasting, but much space for soul-humbling.

Whenever a man proposes to obey in a week's time he confesses himself to be disobedient for that time.

There are no difficulties and obscurities about the Gospel except such as we ourselves create.

I should like you to be able to think about death. If you do not like to think about it at all, my dear friends, I think that there is something wrong in you and you ought to take warning from your own dislike.

We must not judge according to the sight of the eyes or according to present conditions or we shall make gross mistakes.

Till a thing is done men wonder that you think it can be done, and when you have done it they wonder it was never done before.

Propriety hinders very many; decorum is their death. I do not know the precise meaning of it, but there are genteel people about who consider that the finest thing on earth is "propriety."

Gideon was a man of great faith; his name shines among the heroes of great faith in the eleventh chapter of the Epistle to the Hebrews, and you and I will do well if we attain to the same rank in the peerage of faith as he did.

"Well," cries one, "but, you know, we must live." I am not sure about that. There are occasions when it would be better not to live. An old heraldic motto says, "Better death than false of faith."

Feelings are variable as the wind; feelings depend so much upon the body and outward surroundings—so much even upon the condition of the atmosphere. I protest that as to feelings I go up and down very much according to the weather-glass. Therefore I make small account of my feelings.

He is the greatest fool of all who pretends to explain everything, and says he will not believe what he cannot understand.

Those who are washed in the blood of Jesus shall never be drowned in the sea of sorrow.

The best of men are men at the best, and men of strong faith are often men of strong conflicts.

The whole tendency of our holy faith is to elevate and to encourage.

He that is afraid of solemn things has probably solemn reason to be afraid of them.

Jesus will not be your Saviour if you refuse to let Him be your Sovereign. You cannot have half of your Lord.

Our prayer is the shadow of a coming blessing. As "Coming events cast their shadows before them," so, when God is about to bless us, He moves us to pray for that very blessing.

You, dear teachers in the school, may be teaching Luthers and Melanchthons; you may be instructing in those young girls holy women who shall serve the Lord abundantly.

When a man does not pray in the Lord's appointed way, nor through Jesus Christ, nor in dependence upon the Holy Spirit, he does not pray at all. However fine his prayer, it is only a splendid sin.

Thousands have had to weep over their blunder in looking for their heaven on earth; but they follow each other like sheep through a gap, not a bit the wiser for the experience of generations.

Among all the carcasses that shall be washed up on the Dead Sea shore there shall never be found the corpse of Little-faith.

Give us the first seven years of a child with God's grace and we may defy the world, the flesh, and the devil to ruin that immortal soul. Those first years, while yet the clay is soft and plastic, go far to decide the form of the vessel.

He that sitteth on the throne can do for you what you cannot do for yourself, and as He made you once and you became marred by sin He can new-make you, for He saith, "Behold, I make all things new."

The tendency everywhere is to say, "Baptism should not be mentioned; it is sectarian." Who said so? If our Lord commanded it who dares to call it sectarian? We are not commanded to preach a part of the Gospel, but the whole of the Gospel.

Dancing masters and tailors may rig up a fop, but they cannot make a nothing into a man.

He who gets beyond a disciple rises beyond his proper place.

Each one pulls his fellow up or drags him down. Every man in the Church is either a help or a hindrance.

You dream of perfection, but you are a mass of wants and infirmities and conceits, and if it were not for the infinite mercy of God, who deals tenderly with you, you would soon have most painfully to know it to your own dishonor and to the grief of your brethren round about you.

A righteous sentence shall go forth from his mouth who knows not how to flatter the great.

There was a time when Christian people thought it idle to send missionaries to the heathen, but that time only survives in regretful memories.

If we have a special joy in Jesus in any one capacity more than another, let us be joyful in Him as our King.

On taking a survey of our whole life, we see that the kindness of God has run all through it like a silver thread.

We have never reaped such a harvest from any seed as from that which fell from our hand while tears were falling from our eyes.

To have a great many aims and objects is much the same thing as having no aim all; for if a man shoots at many things he will hit none, or none worth the hitting.

Generous souls are made happy by the happiness of others; the money they give to the poor buys them more pleasure than any other that they lay out.

The habit of private prayer and the constant practice of heart-fellowship with the Most High are the surest indicators of the work of the Holy Spirit upon the heart.

The pent-up misery and the seething sin of London may yet produce *a second edition of the French Revolution* unless the grace of God shall interpose.

Think what it will be to have your motives all brought to light; to have it proven that you were godly for the sake of gain; that you were generous out of ostentation or zealous for love of praise; that you were careful in public to maintain a religious reputation, but that all the while everything was done for self and self only.

Do nothing when you are out of temper, and then you will have the less to undo.

If you come to Christ I do not care how you come, for I am sure you could not have come at all if the Father had not drawn you; and if he has drawn you, there is no mistake in your method of coming.

How often have I seen the invalid, who might almost long for death, draw out a long existence of continuous pain, while the man who shook your hand with a powerful grip and stood erect like a column of iron is laid low of a sudden and is gone.

You had better offend a king than one of the Lord's little ones.

To have a hope that you can be a better man is a great help in escaping from sin.

Monsters that revel in darkness must be dragged into the open, that they may be withered up by the light.

Eternal sovereignty is the fountain-head of those gracious decrees in which the Lord hath purposed to do good to the sons of men.

A bad example, a lewd expression, an unholy life, may be the means of drawing others down to perdition; and those that destroy others, and so are soul-murderers, are among the chief of sinners.

After you have believed unto life you will go and do all manner of holy deeds as the result of your new life; but do not attempt them with the view of earning life.

I have no doubt that much sorrow might be prevented if words of encouragement were more frequently spoken fitly and in season; and therefore to withhold them is sin.

"Free grace" we mean still to say, for, as some people will not believe that grace is free, it is still necessary to make it very clear that it is so, and to say not only "grace," but "*free* grace."

It is a sad, sad thing with some men that, the better the Lord deals with them in providence, the worse return they make. On the other hand, there are hearts that turn to the Lord when He smites them.

By the blood of Christ we mean his suffering unto death, the obedience which made him yield His life, and especially the will of His soul to suffer and the object of His mind in suffering.

It is a very remarkable fact, which I have heard asserted by many teachers, that children will learn to read out of the Bible better than from any other book. I scarcely know why; it may, perhaps, be on account of the simplicity of the language; but I believe it is so.

I believe there are thousands of men who could go to the stake and die, or lay their necks on the block to perish with a stroke for Christ, who nevertheless find it hard work to live a holy, consecrated life.

Where do they bury the bad people? Right and left in our church-yard; they seem all to have been the best of folks, a regular nest of saints; and some of them so precious good it is no wonder they died—they were too fine to live in such a wicked world as this.

If you cannot get on honestly, be satisfied not to get on.

Fretful anxiety is forbidden to the Christian.

We are renewed sinners, but we are sinners still.

God cannot manifest himself to us if we continue in sin.

Love thyself less and less and love thy God more.

Faith is that blessed grace which is most pleasing to God.

This present world must be subordinate to the world to come, and is to be cheerfully sacrificed to it if need be.

Your frothy professors quote Dickens or George Eliot, but God's afflicted quote David or Job.

You can sin yourself into an utter deadness of conscience, and that is the first wage of your service of sin.

The one hundred and nineteenth Psalm is a very wonderful composition. Its expressions are many as the waves, but its testimony one as the sea.

Loaded guns and quick-tempered people are dangerous pieces of furniture; they don't mean any hurt, but they are apt to go off and do mischief before you dream of it.

Eternal life must be our possession now; for if we die without it it will never be our possession in the world to come, which is not the state of probation but of fixed and settled reward.

While you are brother to the worm and akin to corruption you are, nevertheless, nearly related to Him who sitteth on the eternal throne.

A deep experience is bound to resort to Scripture for its expression. Human compositions suffice for surface work, but when God's waves and billows have gone over us we quote a Psalm.

I am afraid that many poor souls have remained in darkness, shut in within themselves, when two or three minutes' brotherly cheer might have taken down the shutters and let in the light of day.

There comes a time with a man when it is not so much he that consumes the drink as the drink that consumes him; he is drowned in his cups—sucked down by that which he himself sucked in.

Sometimes our corrupt nature quarrels with God about *our service*. The Lord says, "Go into the Sunday school." "I should have liked to preach," says the young man. "Go into the Sunday school." "Not so, Lord," says he, and he will not go, and thus he misses his life-work. It will not do for us to choose what work we will do.

Teach children practical common-sense home duties as well as the three R's.

We can bear a blow from an enemy, but a wound from our best friend is hard.

The Lord can soon make the gay worldling into the desponding solitary.

Those who boast of perfection will have much to grieve over when once they come to their senses and stand in truth before the living God.

He that delights in God delights not only in God as He is but in all that God does, and this is a higher attainment than some have reached.

I, for one, believe that the more the Word of God has been sifted the more fully has it been confirmed.

We had better abstain from acts which serve no practical purpose, for in this life we have neither time nor strength to waste in fruitless action.

Does he pretend to be a saint? Can he not drink with them as he once did? He is a protest against their excesses, and men don't care for such protests.

How often does it happen that children, though they are not angels, yet are used to do better work than angels could accomplish, for they sweetly lead their parents to God and heaven!

If young men would deny themselves, work hard, live hard, and save in their early days, they need not keep their noses to the grindstone all their lives, as many do.

Rob a Christian of his faith and he will be like Samson when his locks were cut away; the Philistines will be upon him and the Lord will have departed from him.

We are prospering even when we lose our wealth if we grow in grace; but we are in the direst adversity, even if we are growing rich, if we become spiritually poor.

If we are to be acceptable before God there must be no keeping up of favorite sins—no sparing of darling lusts—no providing for secret iniquities; our service will be filthiness before God if our hearts go after our sins.

Some will come into God's house and undertake God's service during the Sabbath day, and yet during the week they are unjust, oppressive, graceless, and greedy—not servants of God, but servants of self and sin.

If there was anything rotten in the state of our salvation we should fear that it would fail us at last. But our foundation is sure, for the Lord has excavated down to the rock; He has taken away every bit of mere sentiment and sham and His salvation is real throughout.

It is ill to be a saint without and a devil within.

We shall be wise to make secular things sacred by trusting them with God.

When desires are so weighty that they burden our words and even crush them down, then are they most prevalent with God.

Good men's memories sometimes fail them.

Life without struggle and difficulty is thin and tasteless. How can a noble life be constructed if there be no difficulty to overcome, no suffering to bear?

You lay it down as a programme that you must be saved in that way or not at all. Is this right? Is this wise? Do you mean to dictate to the Lord?

There is an old nature in us which fights against God still; but the new nature, which is of divine origin, cries after God as a child after its mother.

Let no man think of himself beyond his own experience. Experience is the true gauge; and he who boasts of an untried faith is puffed up with vain glory.

A fuller reward will be ours when the Lord shall come a second time and our bodies shall rise from the grave to share in the glorious reign of the descended King. Then in our perfect manhood we shall behold the face of Him we love and shall be like Him.

It is a cruel thing to tease quick-tempered people, for, though it may be sport to you, it is death to them; at least, it is death to their peace, and may be something worse.

If thou be a child of God thou wilt as surely pray as a man breathes or as a child cries; thou canst not help it.

No dish ever comes to table which is so nauseous as cold religion. Put it away. Neither God nor man can endure it.

That which made Dr. Guthrie ask for a "bairn's hymn" when he was dying is but an instinct of our nature, which leads us to complete the circle by folding together the ends of life. Childlike things are dearest to old age.

Many matters are real difficulties to young believers which are no difficulties to us who have been longer in the way. You and I could clear up in ten minutes' conversation questions and doubts which cause our uninstructed friends months of misery.

The pendulum swings to and fro, advancing and retreating, but yet there is a real progress made; you cannot see it by watching the pendulum, but up higher on the face of the clock there is evidence of an onward march and of a coming hour. The kingdom of God is coming; righteousness shall prevail.

Better keep out of a quarrel than fight your way through it.

Go from faith to faith and thou shalt receive blessing upon blessing.

Take heed that you do not mistake whims of your own mind for the voice of God.

Methinks one day with Christ was worth a half century with Moses.

You must come into heart contact if you are to influence the man.

If we never doubt till we have cause for doubting our life will be rich with faith.

Some of us owed much to old-experienced Christians in our younger days. I know I did.

The background of the cross is the judgment-seat of Christ.

The best preservative under trial is increased spiritual life.

If we once settled it in our minds that we would trust and not be afraid, what peace we should enjoy!

When we are at our worst let us trust with unshaking faith. Recollect that then is the time when we can most glorify God by faith.

It does us much hurt to judge our neighbors, because it flatters our conceit, and our pride grows quite fast enough without feeding. We accuse others to excuse ourselves.

Faith believes in God when there is nothing to support her but the bare promise.

Poverty wants some things, luxury many things, but covetousness wants all things.

Everybody marks the nightingale above all other birds because she singeth when the other minstrels of the woods are silent and asleep; and thus doth faith praise God under the cloud.

Temporal things shall come to you in such proportion as you would yourself desire them if you were able to know all things and to form a judgment according to infinite wisdom.

I was as restless once as those ever-flying birds which hover over the waters of the Golden Horn at Constantinople. They are never seen to rest, and hence *men call them "lost souls."* Such was I! I found no place for the sole of my foot till I knew the Lord Jesus.

I am not going to say which is first, the new birth or faith or repentance. Nobody can tell which spoke of a wheel moves first; it moves as a whole. The moment the divine life comes into the heart we believe; the moment we believe the eternal life is there. We repent because we believe and believe while we repent.

God still guides His servants when they are willing to be guided.

We sometimes know a great deal too much of what we ought not to know.

Want of prayer is a great want indeed.

Faithfulness requires plain speech.

A man who has been helped out of a very severe trouble cannot forget his deliverer.

Let us never think that we are perfect, so that we have no more to learn.

Doubts and fears ill become the children of God.

Let a man of God get side by side with a youth who knows the Scriptures and he feels "This is fit company for me."

A great mistake is made when we suppose that this life is the time for meting out rewards and punishments.

Grateful love cannot be restrained; it is like fire in the bones. Our heart would break for love if it could not find a means of expressing itself at once.

A man who does not look well to his own concerns is not fit to be trusted with other people's. Lots of folks are so busy abroad that they have no time to look at home.

When a man's religion all lies in his saving his own self and in enjoying holy things for his own self there is a disease upon him.

Endurance works in the child of God a close clinging to God, which produces near and dear communion with Him.

We count the thought of the present moment to be methodical madness, Bedlam out of doors; and those who are furthest gone in it are credulous beyond imagination.

There is no dynasty to follow His dynasty; no successor to take up the crown of our Melchisedec. My immortal spirit rejoices in the hope of rendering endless homage to the eternal King.

That atheistic philosophy which makes the whole world to be a chance production which grew of itself, or developed itself by some innate force, is a very dreary piece of fiction to the man who delights himself in the Almighty.

Let us look back upon the whole of our past lives at this hour with a careful, leisurely glance, and see whether there is not enough in our diaries to condemn our doubts and bury our cares, or at least to shut up our anxieties in a cage made of the golden bars of past mercy and fastened in with jeweled bolts of gratitude.

Hypocrites of all sorts are abominable.

God sends the right messenger to the right man.

The prayer of earth melts into the praise of heaven.

To grow heavenly we must grow more believing.

He lives most and lives best who is the means of imparting spiritual life to others.

It is enough for a praying heart that it has a hearing God.

The worst sort of clever men are those who know better than the Bible, and are so learned that they believe that the world had no Maker, and that men are only monkeys with their tails rubbed off.

We are to win influence over our fellow-men by an upright character and a generous behavior.

This century's philosophy will one day be spoken of as an evidence that softening of the brain was very usual among its scientific men.

If, in God's sense of the term, a man really *prays* we may know of a surety that he has passed from death unto life.

If we are always ready for the Master's work we shall be surprised to find how beautifully he makes us fit in with His providence and His grace.

He who, when he receives a message, delivers it at once, with the impression of his call fresh upon him, will deliver it with authority and power.

At home we are unloaded of the world's huge load; the tradesman takes off his apron, the warrior his harness, the bearer his yoke, for he is at home; and if a man may rest anywhere on earth, it must surely be in his own habitation.

Despondency, sickness, bereavement, loss, and even temporal death may fall upon the chosen as visitations of God to deliver them from the power of Satan.

The Lord oftens brings His people away from their sins by giving them sharp and cutting experiences of what evil will do for them. If such be the present consequences of sin, they begin to guess what sin will bring them when they come into judgment and condemnation.

There is a judgment passing upon nations, for as nations will not exist as nations in another world, they have to be judged and punished in this present state. The thoughtful reader of history will not fail to observe how sternly this justice has dealt with empire after empire when they have become corrupt.

That we live, is miraculous; that we die, is natural.

Hearts that have often been traversed by the Gospel become like iron beneath its tread.

If Christians are to be comforters they must learn the art of comforting by being themselves tried.

In 1865, Mr. Spurgeon, while on a visit to Hull, in Yorkshire, during the summer wrote the following poem:

MARRIED LOVE.—TO MY WIFE.

Over the space that parts us, my wife,
  I'll cast me a bridge of song;
Our hearts shall meet, O joy of my life,
  On its arch unseen but strong.

* * * * *

The wooer his new love's name may wear
  Engraved on a precious stone;
But in my heart thine image I wear;
  That heart has long been thine own.

The glowing colors on surface laid
  Wash out in a shower of rain;
Thou need'st not be of rivers afraid,
  For my love is dyed ingrain.

And as every drop of Garda's lake
  Is tinged with sapphire's blue,
So all the powers of my mind partake
  Of joy at the thought of you.

The glittering dewdrops of dawning love
  Exhale as the day grows old,
And fondness, taking the wings of a dove,
  Is gone like a tale of old.

But mine for thee, from the chambers of joy,
  With strength came forth as the sun,
Nor life nor death shall its force destroy—
  Forever its course shall run.

All earth-born love must sleep in the grave,
  To its native dust return;
What God hath kindled shall death outbrave
  And in heaven itself shall burn.

Beyond and above the wedlock tie
  Our union to Christ we feel,
Uniting bonds which were made on high
  Shall hold us when earth shall reel.

Though He who chose us all worlds before
  Must *reign* in our hearts alone,
We fondly believe that we shall adore
  Together before His throne.

Blessed is the man who has many spiritual children born to God under his ministry, for his converts are his defense.

Let us not become men-pleasers, nor grieve inordinately because unreasonable persons are not satisfied with us.

What a breath of peace cools the forehead of the man who remembers that he may pray, and that prayer is heard in heaven.

Worldlings may like a Christian for certain externals; they may admire him for certain advantages they get from him; but as a Christian they cannot love him.

We cannot comfort others if we have never been comforted ourselves. I have heard—and I am sure that it is so—that there is no comforter for a widow like one who has lost her husband.

The devil does not mind having half your heart. He is quite satisfied with that, because he is like the woman to whom the child did not belong; he does not mind if it be cut in halves.

Some people have just enough religion to make them miserable. If they had none, they would be able to enjoy the world; but they have too much religion to be able to enjoy the world, and yet not enough to enjoy the world to come.

The man who does in reality what he seems to do; the man who says what he means and means what he says; the man who is truthful, artless, and sincere in all his general dealings, both before God and man—he it is whose conduct leads us to hope that the light of grace shines within.

Fret not over your heavy troubles, for they are the heralds of weighty mercies.

Wherein I sin, that is my own; but wherein I act rightly, that is of God, wholly and completely.

Graces unexercised are as sweet perfumes slumbering in the cups of the flowers.

None can make "a ring" or "a corner" over the commodity of heavenly truth.

No ignorance is so terrible as ignorance of the Saviour.

Good men suffer when they are tempted, and the better they are the more they suffer.

To have to fight this life-battle without Christ is sure defeat.

If I had to die like a dog I should still wish to live the life of a Christian.

The tendency of the human mind is to idolatry.

God loves truth, and so do those who are renewed in heart.

All God's servants belong to you all, and you must get all the good you can out of them.

You are in Christ, and the Saviour saves you from your sins, but He has not promised that you shall have no sorrow.

The Lord Jesus never overdrives a lame sheep, but He sets the bone and carries the sheep on his shoulders, so tenderly compassionate is He.

We should want to tarry here for ever, and say, "Lo, this is my home," if it were not that an unkind world gives us aliens' treatment and forces us to feel that here we are in exile.

If you see Jesus and abide in the light of His countenance habitually your faces, your characters, your lives, will grow resplendent, even without your knowing it.

Do not attempt to go sneaking to heaven along some back lane; come into the King's highway; take up your cross and follow Him. I would persuade you to an open confession.

There went a man out of this place one evening who was spoken to by one of our friends, who happened to know him in trade and had him in good repute. "What! have you been to hear our minister to-night?" The good man answered, "Yes, I am sorry to say I have." "But," said our friend, "why are you sorry?" "Why," he said, "he has turned me inside out and spoiled my idea of myself. When I went into the Tabernacle I thought I was the best man in Newington, but now I feel that my righteousness is worthless.

By passing through death our Lord has made a thoroughfare for us. We take death and the grave in transit now; they do not hinder our advance to glory and immortality and eternal life.

The love of God the Father is a treasure-house of peace.

To live without Christ is not life, but a breathing death.

The cross which the Lord appoints you has no result but your good.

Your Lord, among the treasures that He gives you, grants a cross.

Read the Bible carefully, and then meditate and meditate and meditate.

We shall not win success unless we hunt for it by careful lives.

We cannot be too careful of our conduct if we aspire to be used of the Lord.

He that has prayed for his breakfast values the providence which sent it.

The Lord is very sensitive to the sorrows of His chosen and very quick to help them.

The man who begins to exult over his fallen brother is the likeliest man to fall himself.

Do not treat God's promises as if they were curiosities for a museum, but use them as every-day sources of comfort.

Carnal objects are not helps to spiritual worship; they are snares to the mind and lead the heart away from God.

The word of God is not defeated. Philosophy and heresy are in league and they gather their armies in haste. The Lord shall make them as the sheaves of the threshing-floor.

If you ask, "What is the highest wisdom upon the earth?" it is to believe in Jesus Christ, whom God has sent—to become His follower and disciple, to trust Him and imitate Him.

It is an empty heart that the devil enters. You know how the boys always break the windows of empty houses; and the devil throws stones wherever the heart is empty.

As workmen are moved to be more diligent in service when they hear their master's footfall, so, doubtless, saints are quickened in their devotion when they are conscious that He whom they worship is drawing near. He has gone away to the Father for a while, and so He has left us alone in this world; but He has said, "I will come again and receive you unto Myself," and we are confident that He will keep His word. John 14:1-3

Deliverance from pride will be a lasting gain to us.

We have been "bought with a price," and henceforth we put in no claim to ourselves, for we belong absolutely to the Lord who bought us. 1 Cor. 6:19-20

The heart must be set upon its design. See how a child cries! Though I am not fond of hearing it, yet I note that *some children cry all over;* when they want a thing, they cry from the tips of their toes to the last hair of their heads. That is the way to preach, and that is the way to pray, and that is the way to live; the whole man must be heartily engaged in holy work.

One thing I have made up my mind to: whether I find present joy or present sorrow, present commendation or present censure, I will be faithful to my Lord.

Only love seeks after love. If I desire the love of another it can surely only be because I myself have love toward him. We care not to be loved by those whom we do not love. It were an embarrassment rather than an advantage to receive love from those to whom we would not return it. When God asks human love, it is because God is love.

The man who has seen affliction when he is blessed of God has the disposition to cheer those who are afflicted.

"Enter into thy closet, and when thou hast shut to the door, pray to thy Father that seeth in secret." That shutting of the door means that we are to seek secrecy and to prevent interruption. Col. 4:2; Matt. 6:5; 1 Thes. 5:17

Temptation to sin is no sin, for in Him was no sin, and yet He was tempted. If you yield to the temptation, therein is sin; but the mere fact that you are tempted, however horrible the temptation, is no sin of yours.

1 Cor. 10:13; 5-15

I have been slenderly cheered by a large number of brethren who have greatly sympathized with me and helped me to fight the Lord's battles by bravely looking on.

I have not a word to say against that scriptural prudence which bids us, like the ant, lay by in store for wintry times; but of the hunger to be rich, and of the selfish expenditure which forgets entirely that our substance is to be used for the glory of God, and that we are only stewards.

If the second advent was to be a spiritual manifestation, to be perceived by the minds of men, the phraseology would be "Every mind shall perceive Him." But it is not so; we read, "Every eye shall see Him." Now, the mind can behold the spiritual, but the eye can only see that which is distinctly material and visible. The Lord Jesus Christ will not come spiritually, for in that sense He is always here; but He will come really and substantially, for every eye shall see Him, even those unspiritual eyes which gazed on Him with hate and pierced Him.

The man that abhors evil and injustice; the man that would do good if it cost him his earthly all; the man who would not do wrong though the world should be his reward for doing it—this is the man who walks in the light, and he is the man that shall have fellowship with God and a sense of cleansing from sin.

You that are tempted of the devil; you that are troubled by mysterious whisperings in your ear; you that, when you sing or pray, have a blasphemy suggested to you; you that even in your dreams start with horror at the thoughts that cross your minds, be comforted, for your Lord knows all about temptation!

The God who is better to you than all your fears, yea, better than your hopes, perhaps intends the affliction to remain with you until *it lifts the latch of heaven for you* and lets you into your eternal rest.

In days to come you will bless God for the clouds and the darkness, since through them your tried faith grew into strong faith and your strong faith ripened into full assurance. Doubtless faith will make our nights the fruitful mothers of brighter days.

A profession of scepticism is often nothing more than the whistling of the boy as he goes through the church-yard and is afraid of ghosts, and therefore "whistles hard to keep his courage up." They try to get rid of the thought of God because of that ghost of conscience which makes cowards of them all.

Perhaps we put too much of our own explanation with the Lord's own word; perhaps we have thought that clever illustrations were needful, and so have overlaid the truth with our poor imagination.

One Paul standing in the sinking ship saves all from ruin by the majesty of his immovable courage; and one Christ—such a Christ as ours—in the midst of a church turns a horde of cowards into an army of heroes.

There is an essential difference between man's word and God's word, and it is fatal to mistake the one for the other. If you receive even the Gospel as the word of man you cannot get the blessing out of it, for the sweetness of the Gospel lies in the confidence of our heart that this is the Word of God.

Faith is not merely believing facts but trusting to a person. God has set forth Christ to be a propitiation for sin; He becomes to me my propitiation when I trust Him.

I remember a man, born blind, who loved our Lord most intensely, and he was wont to glory in this, that his eyes had been reserved for his Lord. Said he, "The first whom I shall ever see will be the Lord Jesus Christ. The first sight that greets my newly-opened eyes will be the Son of Man in his glory."

To my mind it is one of the most delightful truths of Scripture, though so much neglected, that God's people are in covenant with God by a covenant of grace.

We still get far too fond of the world.

We are never without a Providence to observe.

It is a happy day when a full Christ and empty sinners meet.

God buries His workmen but His work goes on.

God will not have fellowship with any whose minds are crooked and deceitful.

Those who speak lightly of faith are of a different mind from the Lord.

Wherever there is a self-satisfaction which is afraid of light we suspect that the rat of hypocrisy is not far off.

We are sorry for the friendless, but none are so forlorn as those who have not Jesus for a friend.

When the world pretends to love, understand that it now hates you more cordially than ever and is carefully baiting its trap to catch you and ruin you.

It was said once of the whole world that it was nothing better than a prison for the man who had offended Cæsar; and I may say of the great universe, however wide it be, that it is but a narrow cell for the man who has offended God.

The wicked shall find that there are special sorrows for them—whips of scorpions for them, especially when they get farther on in life, and their youthful fires burn down to a black ash. Woe unto sinners when they have to reap the fruits of their evil deeds!

Have you a friend to whom you wish to make a present? I know what you do—you try to find out what that friend would value, for you say, "I should like to give him what would please him." Do you want to give God something that is sure to please Him? You need not build a church of matchless architecture; I do not know that God cares much about stones and wood. You need not wait till you shall have amassed money to endow a row of almshouses. It is well to bless the poor, but Jesus said that one who gave two mites, which made a farthing, gave more than all the rich men who cast in of their wealth into the treasury. What would God my Father like me to give? He answers, "My son, give Me thine heart." He will be pleased with that, for He Himself seeks the gift.

It is a pleasant sight to see anybody thanking God; for the air is heavy with the hum of murmuring, and the roads are dusty with complaints and lamentations.

The God of all grace has ways of getting at human hearts when to our thinking every avenue is fast closed.

Some men would wish to have themselves written down at a very high figure, but a cipher is quite sufficient.

The best saints are poor things; and as for some of us who are not the best, what poor, poor things we are.

We have those around us who seem to think that great grace can only display itself by raving and raging. The religion of the quiet Jesus was never intended to drive us to the verge of insanity.

Surely there is more righteousness in trusting the Lord than in all the works of the flesh.

Go not away and dream, and say to yourself, "Oh, there is some spiritual meaning about all this."

What a discovery it will be when, having struggled through one life of sorrow, you shall find yourself beginning another life of greater sorrow, which will never come to an end.

There will come to godly men, sometimes, *temptations to sin*. The purest have been tempted to impurity; the most devout have been tempted to blaspheme; men full of integrity have been tempted to dishonesty, and the most truthful to falsehood.

The devil's work is never done; one word from the Lord, and it is all undone in a trice.

Certain men never get on in business; they do not like their trade, and so they never prosper. And certainly, in the matter of religion, no man can ever prosper if he does not love it, if his whole heart is not in it.

Of all the devils in the world I hate a roaring devil least; but a fawning devil is the worst devil that ever a man meets.

Young men and women usually feel great interest in their fathers' lifestory—if it be a worthy one—and what they hear from them of their personal experience of the goodness of God will abide with them.

It were a blessed thing to go through fifty hells to heaven if such a thing could be.

Weakness hurries, rages, shouts, for it has need to do so. Strength moves with its own deliberate serenity and effects its purpose.

You grow uneasy because near two thousand years have passed since His ascension, and Jesus has not yet come; but you do not know what had to be arranged for, and how far the lapse of time was absolutely necessary for the Lord's design. Those are no little matters which have filled up the great pause; the intervening centuries have teemed with wonders.

Live upon Christ, who is the daily manna, and you will live well.

Oh! if ever a man ought to cling to Christ more than at any other time, it is when he is poor.

I am sometimes startled at the power of a feeble prayer to win a speedy answer.

Christ is not the cause of divine love, but the sweetest and best fruit of it.

As we love the souls of men, we will spend our last breath in the defense of our Lord's substitution.

The life of a genuine Christian is a perpetual miracle, which could be wrought by none but the Lord God.

Any man can sing when his cup is full of delights; the believer alone has songs when waters of a bitter cup are wrung out to him.

The believer in the world finds himself like wheat under the flail, for so the text puts it, "In the world you shall have tribulation."

When ungodly men are tempted the bait is to their taste, and they swallow it greedily. Temptation is a pleasure to them; indeed, they sometimes tempt the devil to tempt them.

The joy of salvation to us in that we are delivered from this present evil world, delivered from the lusts of the flesh, delivered from the old death of natural corruption, delivered from the power of Satan, and from the dominion of evil.

What our boys need in starting in this life is a God; if we have nothing else to give them, they have enough if they have God. What our girls want in quitting the nurture of home is God's love in their hearts, and whether they have fortunes or not is a small matter.

Now you are content to be a Christian; satisfied to mix with poor people in holy service; quite pleased at an opportunity of teaching in a ragged school. Ah! but there may come a moment when Satan will show you the kingdoms of this world, and he will say, "All these will I give thee if thou wilt fall down and worship me;" and you may feel as if the service of Christ was not, after all, very respectable; that you could do better in the world; find choicer company, enter more select society. But drive, drive these carrion-crows away.

It is quite clear that men will not be universally converted when Christ comes, because if they were so they would not wail.

Thanks be unto God for the tribulation which weans our thoughts from earth, and wins them for heaven, and let all the people say, "Amen."

I would not have to go through life without a Saviour if I might be made an emperor.

His saints shall be caught up together with Him in the clouds, to meet the Lord in the air; but to those who shall remain on earth the clouds shall turn their blackness and horror of darkness.

When we meet with God we must be serious and resolute in His worship, and if difficulties arise we must encounter them with all our might, resolving that we will offer to God a sacrifice which shall not be torn by distracting influences.

Human sympathy is the basket of silver to bear to me the golden apples of divine consolation.

The Lord Jesus shall come to earth a second time as literally as He has come a first time.

If an enemy has said anything against your character it will not always be worth while to answer him. Silence has both dignity and argument in it.

I remember that a person came to me once and told me that she had prayed for affliction. I replied, "Dear soul, dear soul, do not be so foolish. You will have quite enough trouble without asking for it."

Every hour that you listen to the Gospel and bar your heart against it you are less and less likely to admit it.

There are no two exactly alike in all the family of God, and yet the likeness to the Elder Brother is to be seen more or less in each one.

A congregation is a strange aggregate; it is like the gatherings of a net or the collections of a dredge. If it is a very large one it is specially remarkable. If anybody could write the histories of all gathered here the result would be a library of singular stories.

There are ten thousand gates to death. One man is choked by a grape-stone, another dies through sleeping in a newly whitewashed room; one receives death as he passes by a reeking sewer, another finds it in the best kept house or by a chill taken in a walk. Those who study neither to eat nor to drink anything unwholesome, nor go into quarters where the arrows of death are flying, yet pass away on a sudden, falling from their couch into a coffin, from their seat into the sepulchre.

There is such a thing as carrying the cross till you are so accustomed to it that you would be almost uneasy without it.

There cannot be anything comparable in the world to the service of God.

Temptation is a mark of sonship rather than any reflection thereupon.

I cast myself upon the Lord alone, willing to be forsaken of all for the truth's sake.

A lie to our fellow-men is meanness; but a lie to God is madness.

Enjoy the calm of heart which comes of knowing that the reserves of God are infinite, and that at any moment they can come and deliver us should an emergency occur.

There cannot be anything so worthy of your noblest manhood as to be truly the disciples of the Lord Jesus Christ.

I knew a young lady—I think I know several of that sort now—whose heart I could never see. I could not make out why she was so flighty, giddy, frothy, till I discovered that she had kept her heart in a wardrobe. A poor prison for an immortal soul, is it not?

Many of God's people, by reason of a strong faith, are happier in their adversity than they were in their prosperity.

You may come to beggary yet with all your inheritance if you cast off the fear of the Lord and fall into sin.

When the pure Gospel is not preached God's people are robbed of the strength which they need in their life-journey.

You can idolize a minister, you can idolize a poet, you can idolize a patron; but in so doing you break the first and greatest of the commandments and you anger the Most High. He declares Himself to be a jealous God, and He will not yield His throne to another.

To-day they deceive the people with the idle dream of repentance and restoration after death, a fiction unsupported by the least tittle of Scripture.

When young men see an excellent person like you, so moral and amiable, without religion, they gather from your example that godliness is not absolutely needful, and take license to do without it. Thus you may be a curse where you little suspect it; you may be encouraging others in the attempt to live without the Saviour.

He that receives Christ also receives Christ's words.

John warns us that if we *say* that which our characters do not support we lie.

Children of light may for a time walk in the darkness of sorrow.

Personal piety is the backbone of success in the service of God.

To the untruthful mind the genuine is an invitation to be the counterfeit.

A religion which we will not submit to the test of examination cannot be worth much.

Between saying and being, between saying and doing, there may be all the difference in the world.

The sacrifice of the Only-Begotten is the unique hope of sinners.

It is an awful thing for a man to go from hell to hell; to make this world a hell and then find another hell in the next world!

Those of us who can look back upon godly ancestors now in heaven must feel that many ties bind us to follow the same course of life.

If you did not find salvation in Him, then you would find that if earth cannot be heaven it can become marvelously like it.

Our mistakes and blunders in the work usually originate in faults in the closet, faults in the family, faults in our own souls. If we were better our works would be better.

Were you never startled with this, that if, in the preaching of the Gospel to-day, we were to bring to the Lord Jesus a person of high rank and another of the very lowest extraction, they have the same experience and upon the greatest of subjects they talk in the same way? "Oh, but," you say, "they pick up certain phrases." No, no! They differ in speech; the likeness is in heart and character. I frequently meet with converts who have not attended this place of worship more than half a dozen times, but they have been converted, and when they come to tell the story of their inner life you would suppose that they had been born and bred among us and had learned all our ways, for, though they do not use the phrases we use, yet they say the same things. The fact is, we are all alike lost and ruined, and we are born again in the same way, and we find the Saviour in the same way, and we rejoice in Him when we do find Him after much the same fashion and express ourselves very much after the same style.

No man can be illustrious before the Lord unless his conflicts be many. there is much to be said about the pleading of an unhappy heart, compared with the repetitions of one who prays using the same phrases over & over. Distress produces originality of the soul.

O child of God, death hath lost its sting, because the devil's power over it is destroyed! Then cease to fear dying.

Christ Jesus is gold without alloy—light without darkness—glory without cloud.

Doubts are dreary things in times of sorrow. Like wasps they sting the soul.

As warm as is His love to sinners, so hot is His hatred of sin; as perfect as is His righteousness, so complete shall be the destruction of every form of wickedness.

Love is an exotic; it is not a plant which will flourish naturally in human soil, it must be watered from above.

One word of God is like a piece of gold, and the Christian is the gold-beater, and can hammer that promise out for whole weeks.

We see in Simon's carrying the cross a picture of the work of the Church throughout all generations; she is the cross-bearer after Jesus.

Christ exempts you from sin, but not from sorrow. Remember that, and expect to suffer.

It is a Christian's duty to force his way into the inner circle of saintship.

Family worship is beyond measure important, both for the present and succeeding generations.

Christ was "not of the world;" His life and His testimony were a constant protest against conformity with the world.

The Christian should never think or speak lightly of unbelief.

Christian! it is contrary to every promise of God's precious Word that thou shouldst ever be forgotten or left to perish.

It is one of the arrangements of divine Providence that day and night shall not cease, either in the spiritual or natural creation, till we reach the land of which it is written, "There is no night there."

To be with Jesus, in the rest which remaineth for the people of God, is a cheering hope indeed, and to expect this glory so soon is a double bliss.

Our griefs cannot mar the melody of our praise; we reckon them to be the bass part of our life's song.

All alterations and amendments of the Lord's own Word are defilements and pollutions.

Christian, meditate much on heaven; it will help thee to press on, and to forget the toil of the way.

The nearer a man lives to God, the more intensely has he to mourn over his own evil heart; and the more his Master honors him in His service, the more also doth the evil of the flesh vex and tease him day by day.

So deep are our necessities that until we are in heaven we must not cease to pray.

To know God is the highest and best form of knowledge.

It is the easiest thing in the world to give a lenient verdict when one's self is to be tried; but O, be just and true here. Be just to all, but be rigorous to yourself.

The Lord Jesus is a deep sea of joy; my soul shall dive therein, shall be swallowed up in the delights of his society.

God's people are doubly His children; they are His offspring by creation, and they are His sons by adoption in Christ.

Fiery spirits may dash forward over untrodden paths to learn fresh truth and win more souls to Jesus; but some of a more conservative spirit may be well engaged in reminding the Church of her ancient faith and restoring her fainting sons.

What whips of burning wire will be yours when conscience shall smite you with all its terrors!

We can never be too confident when we confide in Him alone, and never too much concerned to *have such* a trust.

Keep the altar of *private prayer* burning. This is the very life of all piety.

When we give our hearts with our alms we give well.

When it is the Lord's work in which we rejoice, we need not be afraid of being too glad.

Cautious pilots have no desire to try how near the quicksand they can sail, or how often they may touch a rock without springing a leak; their aim is to keep as nearly as possible in the midst of a safe channel.

If we indulge in any confidence which is not grounded on the Rock of Ages our confidence is worse than a dream.

Self must stand out of the way that there may be room for God to be exalted.

Let us take the pure gold of thankfulness and the jewels ot praise and make them into another crown for the head of Jesus.

It is marvelous that the Lord should regard those intermittent spasms of importunity which come and go with our necessities.

The graces of the Christian character must not resemble the rainbow in its transitory beauty, but, on the contrary, must be established, settled, abiding.

Have a love to all the saints, and add to that a *charity* which openeth its arms to all men and loves their souls.

We only progress in sound living as we progress in sound understanding.

How unwisely do those believers talk who make preferences in the Persons of the Trinity.

May your character not be a writing upon the sand, but an inscription upon the rock.

Many professors give way to temper as though it were useless to attempt resistance; but let the believer remember that he must be a conqueror in every point or else he connot be crowned.

If those who spend so many hours in idle company, light reading, and useless pastimes could learn wisdom they would find more profitable society and more interesting engagements in meditation than in the vanities which now have such charms for them.

We should all know more, live nearer to God, and grow in grace, if we were more alone. Meditation chews the cud and extracts the real nutriment from the mental food gathered elsewhere.

We know that our enemies are attempting impossibilities. They seek to destroy the eternal life which cannot die while Jesus lives, to overthrow the citadel against which the gates of hell shall not prevail.

Trouble does not necessarily bring consolation with it to the believer, but the presence of the Son of God in the fiery furnace with him fills his heart with joy.

The soldier fights for his captain and is crowned in his captain's victory, so the believer contends for Christ and gets his triumph out of the triumphs of his Master.

As love comes from heaven, so it must feed on heavenly bread. It cannot exist in the wilderness unless it be fed by manna from on high. Love must feed on love. The very soul and life of our love to God is His love to us.

Fair is that lone star which smiles through the rifts of the thunder-clouds; bright is the oasis which blooms in the wilderness of sand; so fair and so bright is love in the midst of wrath.

If every day I journeyed towards the goal of my desires I should soon reach it, but backsliding leaves me still far off from the prize of my high calling and robs me of the advances which I had so laboriously made.

The assumed appearance of superior sanctity frequently accompanies a total absence of all vital godliness. The saint in public is a devil in private.

"I am a Roman!" was of old a reason for integrity; far more, then, let it be your argument for holiness, "I am Christ's."

Go to the river of thine experience and pull up a few bulrushes and plait them into an ark, wherein thine infant faith may float safely on the stream. Forget not what thy God has done for thee.

Death's darts are under the Lord's lock, and the grave's prisons have divine power as their warder.

No one else shall have thy portion; it is reserved in heaven for thee, and thou shalt have it ere long, for there shall be no vacant thrones in glory when all the chosen are gathered in.

You will not find on this side of heaven a holier people than those who receive into their hearts the doctrine of Christ's righteousness.

"I will be their God." This is the masterpiece of all the promises; its enjoyment makes a heaven below, and will make a heaven above.

Jesus is to believers the one pearl of great price, for whom we are willing to part with all that we have. He has so completely won our love that it beats alone for Him; to His glory we would live, and in defense of His gospel we would die; He is the pattern of our life and the model after which we would sculpture our character.

This alone is the true life of a Christian—its source, its sustenance, its fashion, its end, all gathered up in one word—*Christ Jesus*.

There is a perfection yet to be realized, which is sure to all the seed. Is it not delightful to look forward to the time when every stain of sin shall be removed from the believer and he shall be presented faultless before the throne, without spot, or wrinkle, or any such thing?

Did you lose Christ by sin? You will find Christ in no other way but by the giving up of the sin and seeking by the Holy Spirit to mortify the member in which the lust doth dwell. Did you lose Christ by neglecting the Scriptures? You must find Christ in the Scriptures. It is a true proverb, "Look for a thing where you dropped it; it is there." So look for Christ where you lost Him, for He has not gone away.

The seasons change and thou changest, but thy Lord abides evermore the same, and the streams of His love are as deep, as broad, and as full as ever.

Blessed is death, since it, through the divine power, disrobes us of this work-day garment to clothe us with the wedding garment of incorruption.

No greater eagerness will ever be seen among satanic tormentors than in that day when devils drag the hypocrite's soul down to perdition.

Come what may, God's people are safe. Let convulsions shake the solid earth, let the skies themselves be rent in twain, yet amid the wreck of worlds the believer shall be as secure as in the calmest hour of rest.

Believers who know Christ understand that delight and faith are so blessedly united that the gates of hell cannot prevail to separate them.

Ungodly persons and mere professors never look upon religion as a joyful thing; to them it is service, duty, or necessity, but never pleasure or delight.

The old nature is very active, and loses no opportunity of plying all the weapons of its deadly armory against new-born grace; while, on the other hand, the new nature is ever on the watch to resist and destroy its enemy.

I would have all those that hear of my great deliverance from hell and my most blessed visitation from on high laugh for joy with me.

When the soul shall have understanding to discern all the Saviour's gifts, wisdom wherewith to estimate them, and time in which to meditate upon them, such as the world to come will afford us, we shall then commune with Jesus in a nearer manner than at present.

Let us not imagine that *the soul* sleeps in insensibility. "To-day shalt thou be with me in Paradise," is the whisper of Christ to every dying saint.

Ours are its gates of pearl and walls of chrysolite; ours the azure light of the city that needs no candle nor light of the sun; ours the river of the water of life and the twelve manner of fruits which grow on the trees planted on the banks thereof; there is nought in heaven that belongeth not to us. "Things present, or things to come," all are ours.

Be content to live unknown for a little while, and to walk your weary way through the fields of poverty or up the hills of affliction, for by and by you shall reign with Christ.

Sleep makes each night a Sabbath for the day. Sleep shuts fast the door of the soul and bids all intruders tarry for awhile that the life within may enter its summer garden of ease. The toil-worn believer quietly sleeps as does the weary child when it slumbers on its mother's breast.

Morning devotion anchors the soul, so that it will not very readily drift far away from God during the day.

Past experiences are doubtful food for Christians; a present coming to Christ alone can give us joy and comfort.

As the highest portraiture of Jesus, try to forgive your enemies as He did.

Bad nursing in their spiritual infancy often causes converts to fall into a despondency from which they never recover.

We know of no cure for the love of evil in a Christian like abundant intercourse with the Lord Jesus.

When the night lowers and the tempest is coming on the Heavenly Captain is always closest to His crew.

It is a sweet thought that Jesus Christ did not come forth without His Father's permission, authority, consent, and assistance.

Every individual believer is precious in the sight of the Lord; a shepherd would not lose one sheep, nor a jeweler one diamond, nor a mother one child, nor a man one limb of his body, nor will the Lord lose one of His redeemed people.

Above all other seasons a man needs his God when his heart is melted within him because of heaviness.

Quail not before superior numbers, shrink not from difficulties or impossibilities, flinch not at wounds or death, smite with the two-edged sword of the Spirit and the slain shall lie in heaps.

Sin a little thing? It girded the Redeemer's head with thorns and pierced His heart! It made *Him* suffer anguish, bitterness, and woe. Could you weigh the least sin in the scales of eternity you would fly from it as from a serpent and abhor *the least appearance of evil.*

The devils are united as one man in their infamous rebellion, while we believers in Jesus are divided in our service of God and scarcely ever work with unanimity.

The breath of morn redolent of the smell of flowers is incense offered by earth to her Creator, and living men should never let the dead earth excel them.

Think not that a long period intervenes between the instant of death and the eternity of glory. When the eyes close on earth they open in heaven.

We should as soon think of printing a form for our children to use in addressing their parents as draw up a form to be offered to our Father who is in heaven.

As for His failing you, never dream of it—hate the thought. The God who has been sufficient until now should be trusted to the end.

He who rushes from his bed to his business and waiteth not to worship is as foolish as though he had not put on his clothes or cleansed his face, and as unwise as though he dashed into battle without arms or armor.

We remain on earth as sowers to scatter good seed, as plowmen to break up the fallow ground, as heralds publishing salvation. We are here as the "salt of the earth," to be a blessing to the world. We are here to glorify Christ in our daily life. We are here as workers for Him, and as "workers together with Him."

May the horrible trinity of the world, the flesh, and the devil never overcome us.

We have good reason, indeed, for hating evil when we look back and trace its deadly workings. Such mischief did evil do us that our souls would have been lost had not omnipotent love interfered to redeem us.

Our prayers and efforts cannot make us ready for heaven apart from the hand of Jesus, who fashioneth our hearts aright.

Let us charge ourselves to bind a heavenly forget-me-not about our hearts for Jesus our Beloved, and whatever else we let slip let us hold fast to Him.

It is the incessant turmoil of the world, the constant attraction of earthly things, which takes away the soul from Christ.

The Christian knows no change with regard to God. He may be rich to-day and poor to-morrow; he may be sickly to-day and well to-morrow; he may be in happiness to-day, to-morrow he may be distressed—but there is no change with regard to his relationship to God. If He loved me yesterday, He loves me to-day. My unmoving mansion of rest is my blessed Lord.

Labor to impress thyself with a deep sense of the value of the place to which thou art going. If thou rememberest that thou art going to heaven, thou wilt not sleep on the road. If thou thinkest that hell is behind thee and the devil pursuing thee thou wilt not loiter.

Ye unknown workers, who are occupied for your Lord amid the dirt and wretchedness of the lowest of the low, be of good cheer, for jewels have been found upon dunghills ere now, earthen pots have been filled with heavenly treasure, and ill weeds have been transformed into precious flowers.

He who loves truth must hate every false way.

Far superior to the jealousy, selfishness, and greed, which admit of no participation of their advantages, Christ deems His happiness completed by His people sharing it.

Being born in a Christian land and being recognized as professing the Christian religion is of no avail whatever, unless there be something more added to it—the being "born again" by the power of the Holy Spirit.

We do our Lord an injustice when we suppose that He wrought all his mighty acts and showed Himself strong for those in the early time, but doth not perform wonders or lay bare His arms for the saints who are now upon the earth.

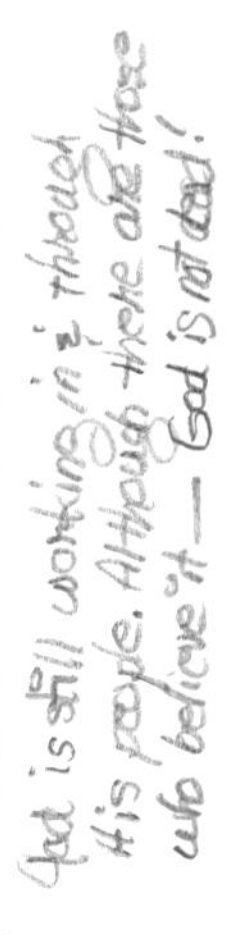

Prayer is the lisping of the believing infant, the shout of the fighting believer, the requiem of the dying saint falling asleep in Jesus. It is the breath, the watchword, the comfort, the strength, and honor of a Christian.

The Holy Spirit makes men penitents long before He makes them divines; and he who believes what he knows shall soon know more clearly what he believes.

As you grow *downward* in humility seek also to grow *upward*, having nearer approaches to God in prayer and more intimate fellowship with Jesus.

Jesus Christ is Himself the sum and substance of the covenant, and as one of its gifts He is the property of every believer.

Desire is insatiable as death, but He who filleth all in all can fill it. The capacity of our wishes who can measure? but the immeasurable wealth of God can more than overflow it.

He who grows not in the knowledge of Jesus refuses to be blessed.

Spiritual light has many beams and prismatic colors, but whether they be knowledge, joy, holiness, or life, all are divinely good.

Let me be on my guard when the world puts on a loving face, for it will, if possible, betray me, as it did my Master, with a kiss.

In our Christian pilgrimage it is well, for the most part, to be looking forward. Forward lies the crown, and onward is the goal. Whether it be for hope, for joy, for consolation, or for the inspiring of our love, the future must, after all, be the grand object of the eye of faith.

You have too frequently had a view of your own heart to dream for a moment of any perfection *in yourself*. But amid this sad consciousness of imperfection, here is comfort for you—you are "perfect *in Christ Jesus*." In God's sight, you are "complete in Him;" *even now* you are "accepted in the beloved."

When a person is dear everything connected with him becomes dear for his sake.

The distance between glorified spirits in heaven and militant saints on earth seems great; but it is not so. We are not so far from home—a moment will bring us there.

Calm endurance answers some questions infinitely more conclusively than the loftiest eloquence.

Abba, Father! He who can say this hath uttered better music than cherubim or seraphim can reach. There is heaven in the depth of that word—Father! There is all I can ask; all my necessities can demand; all my wishes can desire. I have all in all to all eternity when I can say, "Father."

Christian! do not dishonor your religion by always wearing a brow of care.

Whatever thou art, thou hast nothing to make thee proud. The more thou hast, the more thou art in debt to God; and thou shouldst not be proud of that which renders thee a debtor.

Trouble is often the means whereby God delivers us. God knows that our backsliding will soon end in our distruction, and He in mercy sends the rod.

How often are the saints of God downcast and sad! I do not think they ought to be. I do not think they would if they could always see their perfection in Christ.

Here, rest is but partial; *there*, it is *perfect*. *Here*, the Christian is always unsettled; he feels that he has not yet attained. *There*, all are at rest; they have attained the summit of the mountain; they have ascended to the bosom of their God. Higher they cannot go. Ah, toil-worn laborer, only think when thou shalt rest forever.

When a Christian grasps a promise, if he do not take it to God he dishonors Him; but when he hastens to the throne of grace and cries, "Lord, I have nothing to recommend me but this, 'Thou hast said it,'" then his desire shall be granted. Our heavenly Banker delights to cash His own notes.

However difficult and painful thy road, it is marked by the footsteps of thy Saviour; and even when thou reachest the dark valley of the shadow of death, and the deep waters of the swelling Jordan, thou wilt find His footprints there.

We need not teach men to complain; they complain fast enough without any education.

God's promises were never meant to be thrown aside as waste paper; He intended that they should be used. God's gold is not miser's money, but is minted to be traded with. Nothing pleases our Lord better than to see His promises put in circulation; He loves to see His children bring them up to Him and say, "Lord, do as Thou hast promised."

Brother, hush that murmur, natural though it be, and continue a diligent pupil in the College of Content.

If none of God's saints were poor and tried we should not know half so well the consolations of divine grace.

The spade of trouble digs the reservoir of comfort deeper, and makes more room for consolation.

If thou wouldst know the path of duty, take God for thy compass; if thou wouldst steer thy ship through the dark billows, put the tiller into the hand of the Almighty.

Sin will yield to nothing less potent than the blood of Him whom God hath set forth as a propitiation.

This vale of tears is but the pathway to the better country; this world of woe is but the stepping-stone to a world of bliss.

The Ruler of providence bears a pair of scales; in this side He puts His people's trials, and in that He puts their consolations. When the scale of trial is nearly empty you will always find the scale of consolation in nearly the same condition; and when the scale of trial is full you will find the scale of consolation just as heavy.

No promise is of private interpretation. Whatever God has said to any one saint He has said to all. When He opens a well for one it is that all may drink. When He openeth a granary door to give out food, there may be some one starving man who is the occasion of its being opened, but all hungry saints may come and feed too.

If I neglect prayer for never so short a time, I lose all the spirituality to which I had attained; if I draw no fresh supplies from heaven, the old corn in my granary is soon consumed by the famine which rages in my soul.

Just so far as the Lord shall give us grace to suffer *for* Christ, to suffer *with* Christ, just so far does he honor us.

You can recollect the sayings of great men; you treasure up the verses of renowned poets; ought you not to be profound in your knowledge of the words of God, so that you may be able to quote them readily when you would solve a difficulty or overthrow a doubt?

A daily portion is *all that a man really wants*. We do not need to-morrow's supplies; that day has not yet dawned, and its wants are as yet unborn.

Contentment is one of the flowers of heaven, and if we would have it, it must be cultivated; it will not grow in us by nature; it is the new nature alone that can produce it, and even then we must be specially careful and watchful that we maintain and cultivate the grace which God has sown in us.

We have been compelled to go to God for our souls as constant beggars asking for everything. Bear witness, children of God, you have never been able to get anything for your souls elsewhere.

No joy can excel that of the soldier of Christ; Jesus reveals Himself so graciously and gives such sweet refreshment that the warrior feels more calm and peace in his daily strife than others in their hours of rest.

It is quite right to desire to depart, if we can do it in the same spirit that Paul did, because to be with Christ is far better; but the wish to escape from trouble is a selfish one.

Anxiety makes us doubt God's loving-kindness, and thus our love to Him grows cold; we feel mistrust, and thus grieve the Spirit of God, so that our prayers become hindered, our consistent example marred, and our life one of self-seeking.

If thou *wilt* murmur against the chastening, take heed, for it will go hard with murmurers. God always chastises His children twice, if they do not bear the first stroke patiently.

The anvil breaks a host of hammers by quietly bearing their blows.

Rest assured that we have already experienced more ills than death at its worst can cause us.

Whenever a man is about to stab religion he usually professes very great reverence for it. Let me beware of the sleek-faced hypocrisy which is armor-bearer to heresy and infidelity.

He who does not long to know more of Christ knows nothing of Him yet. Whoever hath sipped this wine will thirst for more, for although Christ doth satisfy, yet it is such a satisfaction that the appetite is not cloyed but whetted.

Be thou ever one of those whose manners are Christian, whose speech is like the Nazarene, whose conduct and conversation are so redolent of heaven that all who see you may know that you are the Saviour's, recognizing in you His features of love and His countenance of holiness.

Favorite children are often the cause of much sin in believers; the Lord is grieved when he sees us doting upon them above measure; they will live to be as great a curse to us as Absalom was to David, or they will be taken from us to leave our homes desolate. If Christians desire to grow thorns to stuff their sleepless pillows, let them dote upon their dear ones.

Good for evil, recollect, is godlike.

Every hour has its duty; do thou continue in thy calling as the Lord's servant until He shall suddenly appear in His glory.

Very frequently anger is the madman's firebrand.

Grasp the sweet promises, thresh them out by meditation, and feed on them with joy.

Keep out that monster unbelief.

Learn, dear reader, to glorify the Lord by leaving no means untried, if by using them thou wouldst not dishonor the name of the Lord.

We know not what prayer cannot do!

Every day should be the birthday of the Saviour to a renewed soul.

A goodly man often grows best when his worldly circumstances decay.

Blistered, leprous, filthy lips may touch the stream of divine love; they cannot pollute it, but shall themselves be purified.

He who follows Christ for his bag is a Judas; they who follow for loaves and fishes are children of the devil; but they who attend Him out of love to Himself are His own beloved ones.

You are meddling with Christ's business and neglecting your own when you fret about your lot and circumstances.

If an angel should fly from heaven and inform the saint personally of the Saviour's love to him the evidence would not be one whit more satisfactory than that which is borne in the heart by the Holy Ghost.

Men will attend to the most multiplied and minute ceremonial regulations, for such things are *pleasing to the flesh;* but true religion is too humbling, too heart-searching, too thorough for the tastes of carnal men; they prefer something more ostentatious, flimsy, and worldly.

The first promise ran thus: "*The seed of the woman,*" not the offspring of the man. Since venturous woman led the way in the sin which brought forth Paradise lost, she, and she alone, ushers in the Regainer of Paradise.

Though dishonest as the thief, though unchaste as the woman who was a sinner, though fierce as Saul of Tarsus, though cruel as Manasseh, though rebellious as the prodigal, the great heart of love will look upon the man who feels himself to have no soundness in him, and will pronounce him clean when he trusts in Jesus crucified.

More wealth brings more care, but more grace brings more joy.

Human action is frequently the hasty result of passion or fear, and is followed by regret and alteration.

A man may have too much money or too much honor, but he cannot have too much grace.

If we would be eminently useful, we must not be content with forming schemes in our heart and talking of them; we must practically carry out "*whatsoever our hand findeth to do.*"

One good deed is of more worth than a thousand brilliant theories.

There is no purer or more thrilling delight to be known this side of heaven than that of having Christ's joy fulfilled in us, that our joy may be full.

Tale-bearing emits a threefold poison; for it injures the teller, the hearer, and the person concerning whom the tale is told.

We have no other time in which to live. The past is gone; the future has not arrived; we never shall have any time but time *present*.

The Holy Spirit permits us to censure sin, and prescribes the way which we are to do it. It must be done by rebuking our brother to his face, not by railing behind his back. This course is manly, brotherly, Christ-like, and, under God's blessing, will be useful.

He who wraps a thread-bare coat about a good conscience has gained a spiritual wealth far more desirable than any he has lost.

Saints know that a grain of heart's-ease is of more value than a ton of gold.

Losses, crosses, heaviness, sickness, poverty, and a thousand other ills are of the Lord's sending, and come to us with wise design.

God's smile and a dungeon are enough for a true heart; His frown and a palace would be hell to a gracious spirit.

Satan may worry, but he cannot destroy us.

Our religion is not to be confined to our closet; we must carry out into practical effect that which we believe.

No faith is so precious as that which lives and triumphs in adversity.

It is for home that we work and labor. The thought of it gives strength to bear the daily burden and quickens the fingers to perform the task.

Be most in those engagements which you have experimentally proved to draw you nearer to Christ.

Sin may drag thee ever so low, but Christ's great atonement is still under all. You may have descended into the deeps, but you cannot have fallen so low as "the uttermost;" and to the uttermost He saves.

This is the joy we have to-day, that we are saved in Him; and if this joy be satisfying, wherefore should we think of changing? Who barters gold for dross?

Duplicity is abominable with God, and hypocrisy his soul hateth.

Christ will be all or nothing.

Prayers are instantly noticed in heaven.

Let us move in the common affairs of life with studied holiness, diligence, kindness, and integrity.

A backslider, if there be a spark of life left in him, will groan after restoration.

To forget to praise God is to refuse to benefit ourselves; for praise, like prayer, is one great means of promoting the growth of the spiritual life. It helps to remove our burdens, to excite our hope, to increase our faith.

Praise should always follow answered prayer.

A primary qualification for serving God with any amount of success and for doing God's work well and triumphantly is a sense of our own weakness.

Those who serve God must serve Him in His own way and in His strength or He will never accept their service.

The soul-enriching path of prayer is open to the very weakest saint.

All the strength supplied to us by our gracious God is meant for service.

The nearest place to the gate of heaven is the throne of the heavenly grace.

There is not a promise in the Word which shall be withheld.

Earth hath no words which can set forth the holy calm of a soul leaning on Jesus' bosom.

Our first faith—that simple faith by which, having nothing, we become possessors of all things.

What we have known of our faithful God proves that He will keep us to the end.

Sincere repentance is *continual*. Believers repent until their dying day.

He can labor without present reward who looks for a reward in the world to come.

Some Christians are living *on* Christ, but are not so anxious to live *for* Christ.

To many saints old age is the choicest season in their lives.

How heart-cheering to the believer is the delight which God has in His saints!

From the altar of age the flashes of the fire of youth are gone, but the more real flame of earnest feeling remains.

When we repent of sin we must have one eye upon sin and another upon the cross, or it will be better still if we fix both our eyes upon Christ, and see our transgressions only in the light of His love.

Saints will not be out of place in heaven; their beauty will be as great as that of the place prepared for them.

A true prayer is an inventory of wants, a catalogue of necessities, a revelation of hidden poverty.

Love should give wings to the feet of service and strength to the arms of labor.

Every attribute of God should become a fresh ray in the sunlight of our gladness.

We have the earnest of our inheritance in the comforts of the Spirit, which are neither few nor small. Inheritors of joy forever, we have foretastes of our portion.

Prayer is in itself, apart from the answer which it brings, a great benefit to the Christian.

In the family register of glory the small and the great are written with the same pen.

Present afflictions *tend to heighten future joy.* There must be shades in the picture to bring out the beauty of the lights.

Scripture is a never-failing treasury filled with boundless stores of grace. It is the bank of heaven; you may draw from it as much as you please, without let or hindrance.

The Psalms show us that God's people in olden times were wont to think much of God's actions, and to have a song concerning each of them. So let God's people now rehearse the deeds of the Lord.

We must confess that we are "nothing else but sin," for no confession short of this will be the whole truth; and if the Holy Spirit be at work with us, convincing us of sin, there will be no difficulty about making such an acknowledgment—it will spring spontaneously from our lips.

The best of men are conscious, above all others, that they are men at the best.

We shall never find happiness by looking at our prayers, our doings, or our feelings; it is what *Jesus* is, not what *we* are, that gives rest to the soul.

The jewels of a Christian are his afflictions. The regalia of the kings whom God hath anointed are their troubles, their sorrows, and their griefs.

There is nothing which can so assist you to walk towards heaven with good speed as wearing the image of Jesus on your heart to rule all its motions.

Ah! poor religion, thou has been sorely shot at by cruel foes, but thou hast not been wounded one-half so dangerously by thy foes as by thy friends.

Be content with thine own lot if thou canst not better it, but do not look upon thy neighbor and wish that he were as thyself.

The man who, with pretenses, enters the fold, being nought but a wolf in sheep's clothing, worries the flock more than the lion outside.

Inconsistent professors injure the Gospel more than the sneering critic or the infidel.

It is not *thy hold* of Christ that saves thee—it is Christ; it is not *thy joy* in Christ that saves thee—it is Christ; it is not even faith in Christ, though that be the instrument—it is Christ's blood and merits.

Turn to sacred history and you will find that scarcely ever did a great mercy come to this world unheralded by supplication.

Empty boats float high, but heavily-laden vessels are low in the water; mere professors can boast, but true children of God cry for mercy upon their unprofitableness.

God's people have their trials. It was never designed by God when He chose His people that they should be an untried people.

Wickedness arrays itself in fair garments and imitates the language of holiness, but the precepts of Jesus, like His famous scourge of small cords, chase it out of the temple and will not tolerate it in the church.

Hope itself is like a star—not to be seen in the sunshine of prosperity and only to be discovered in the night of adversity.

God often takes away our comforts and our privileges in order to make us better Christians. He trains His soldiers, not in tents of ease and luxury, but by turning them out and using them to forced marches and hard service. He makes them ford through streams and swim through rivers, and climb mountains and walk many a long mile with heavy knapsacks of sorrow on their backs.

Afflictions are often the black foils in which God doth set the jewels of His children's graces to make them shine the better.

Banquet your faith upon God's own Word, and whatever your fears or wants repair to the Bank of Faith with your Father's note of hand, saying, "Remember the word unto Thy servant, upon which Thou hast caused me to hope."

Be not contented with this unspeakable blessing for thyself alone, but publish abroad the story of the cross. Holy gladness and holy boldness will make you a good preacher, and all the world will be a pulpit for you to preach in.

A Christian should be a striking likeness of Jesus Christ. You have read lives of Christ, beautifully and eloquently written; but the best life of Christ is His living biography, written out in the words and actions of His people.

Some Christians are sadly prone to *look* on the *dark* side of everything, and to dwell more upon what they have gone through than upon what God has done for them.

We have many ungratified desires at present, but soon every wish shall be satisfied, and all our powers shall find the sweetest employment in that eternal world of joy.

Consider the history of the Redeemer's love and a thousand enchanting acts of affection will suggest themselves, all of which have had for their design the weaving of the heart into Christ and the intertwisting of the thoughts and emotions of the renewed soul with the mind of Jesus.

Some men profess a great deal; but we must not believe any one unless we see that his deeds answer to what he says.

There is no weapon half so deadly as a Judas kiss.

If there be one name sweeter than another in a believer's ear it is the name of *Jesus*. Jesus! it is the name which moves the harps of heaven to melody. Jesus! the life of all our joys. If there be one name more charming, more precious than another, it is this name. It is woven into the very warp and woof of our psalmody. Many of our hymns begin with it, and scarcely any that are good for anything end without it. It is the sum total of all delights. It is the music with which the bells of heaven ring; a song in a word; an ocean for comprehension, although a drop for brevity; a matchless oratorio in two syllables; a gathering up of the hallelujahs of eternity in five letters.

The sea is made of drops, the rocks are made of grains; and the sea which divides thee from Christ may be filled with the drops of thy little sins; and the rock which has well nigh wrecked thy bark may have been made by the daily working of the coral insects of thy little sins.

Whatever our morning's need may be, let it like a strong current bear us to the ocean of divine love.

It is fondly imagined by some that it must have involved very special privileges to have been the mother of our Lord, because they suppose that she had the benefit of looking into His very heart in a way in which we cannot hope to do. There may be an appearance of plausibility in the supposition, but not much. We do not know that Mary knew more than others; what she did know she did well to lay up in her heart; but she does not appear from anything we read in the Evangelists to have been a better-instructed believer than any other of Christ's disciples. All that she knew we also may discover. Do you wonder that we should say so? Here is a text to prove it: "The secret of the Lord is with them that fear Him, and He will show them His covenant."

We may not make sure that the Lord will at once remove all disease from those we love, but we may know that believing prayer for the sick is far more likely to be followed by restoration than anything else in the world; and where this avails not, we must meekly bow to His will by whom life and death are determined.

God is oftener in little huts than in rich palaces.

God would have us put on a cheerful courage.

Every position has its duties.

Happy are we if we live in your supplications.

It is not only at the commencement of the Christian life that believers have reason for song; as long as they live they discover cause to sing in the ways of the Lord.

The obedience which God's children yield to Him must be *loving* obedience.

I had need to beware of lean prayers, lean praises, lean duties and lean experiences, for these will eat up the fat of my comfort and peace.

He who cannot calmly leave his affairs in God's hand, but will carry his own burden, is very likely to be tempted to use wrong means to help himself.

Upstarts frequently usurp the highest places, while the truly great pine in obscurity.

The Christian who has learned to live by faith is independent of man, even in temporal things; for his continued maintenance he looks to the Lord his God and to Him alone.

Divine grace can make the coward brave.

It is sweet to die in the Lord; it is a covenant blessing to sleep in Jesus.

Our sanctification is a long and continued process, and we shall not be perfected till we lay aside our bodies and enter within the veil.

As speeds the ship towards the port, so hastes the believer towards the haven of his Saviour's bosom.

Let us not fall into the error of letting our passions and carnal appetites ride in triumph, while our nobler powers walk in the dust.

Praise makes worship complete, and without it the pillar of devotion lacks its capital.

A knowledge of doctrine will tend very much to confirm faith.

Thine acceptance is not in thyself but in thy Lord; thou art as much accepted of God to-day, with all thy sinfulness, as thou wilt be when thou standest before His throne, free from all corruption.

A life of misery is usually the lot of those who are united in marriage, or in any other way of their own choosing, with the men of the world.

While there are distinctions as to the *persons* in the Trinity, there are no distinctions of *honor*.

If we truly love Christ we shall care for those who are loved by Him. Those who are dear to Him will be dear to us.

We are engaged in a great war with the Philistines of evil. *Every weapon within our reach must be used.*

Hold Christian company and you will be kept wakeful by it and refreshed and encouraged to make quicker progress in the road to heaven.

Never blush to own your religion; your profession will never disgrace you; take care you never disgrace *that*.

No prayer is half so hearty as that which comes up from the depths of the soul through deep trials and afflictions.

Death is no longer banishment; it is a return from exile, a going home to the many mansions where the loved ones already dwell.

Faith is the road, but communion with Jesus is the well from which the pilgrim drinks.

Care, even though exercised upon legitimate objects, if carried to excess, has in it the nature of sin.

In order to become spiritually vigorous we must seek the spiritual good of others.

We often find, in attempting to teach others, that we *gain instruction for ourselves*. Rom. 2:21a

What the sun is to the day, what the moon is to the night, what the dew is to the flower, such is Jesus Christ to us.

We do not know what tender sympathies we possess until we try to dry the widow's tears and soothe the orphan's grief.

There are no broken friendships nor blighted prospects in heaven. Poverty, famine, peril, persecution, and slander are unknown there.

All means are good and decorous when faith and love are truly set on winning souls.

We have latent talents and dormant faculties which are brought to light by exercise.

What gracious lessons some of us have learned at sick beds. We went to teach the Scriptures; we came away blushing that we knew so little of them. In our converse with poor saints we are taught the way of God more perfectly for ourselves and get a deeper insight into divine truth.

Our strength for labor is hidden even from ourselves until we venture forth to fight the Lord's battles or to climb the mountains of difficulty.

Art thou afraid of hell? He has barred it against the advent of any of His children; they shall never see the gulf of perdition. Whatever foes may be before the Christian they are all overcome.

David was an able master of the human heart, because he had been tutored in the best of all schools—the school of heart-felt, personal experience.

May we all have grace to maintain in our own proper way the purity of the Church as being an assembly of believers and not a nation, an unsaved community of unconverted men.

Little faith will save a man, but little faith cannot do great things for God.

Measure our love by our intentions and it is high indeed; 'tis thus, we trust, our Lord doth judge of it.

Prayer cannot draw down answers from God's throne except it be the earnest prayer of the man who believes.

To know Him is "life eternal," and to advance in the knowledge of Him is to increase in happiness.

He who is not angry at transgression becomes a partaker in it.

Our piety is our pleasure, our hope is our happiness, our duty is our delight.

It augurs for us a day of grace when we begin betimes with God; the sanctifying influence of the season spent upon the mount operates upon each succeeding hour.

The life of a believer is a series of miracles wrought by "the mighty God."

Would to God that the daily turmoil were less vehement—that we had more time and heart for praising the name of the Lord.

Your prayers, and your repentances, and your tears—the whole of them put together—are worth nothing apart from Him. "None but Jesus can do helpless sinners good;" or helpless saints either.

Delight and true religion are as allied as root and flower:

The love of Christ in its sweetness, its fullness, its greatness, its faithfulness, passeth all human comprehension.

There is no hope of prevalence with God unless we abase ourselves that He may exalt us in due time.

The common mercies we enjoy all sing of love, just as the sea-shell, when we put it to our ears, whispers of the deep sea whence it came; but if we desire to hear the ocean itself, we must not look at every-day blessings, but at the transactions of the crucifixion.

There will be no doubt about his having chosen *you* when you have chosen *Him*.

Religion is calculated to give a man happiness below as well as bliss above.

Absence from Christ is hell; but the presence of Jesus is heaven.

No Christian has enjoyed perpetual prosperity; no believer can always keep his harp from the willows.

Winds and waves will not spare us, but they all obey Him; and, therefore, whatever squalls may occur without, faith shall feel a blessed calm within.

If Christ were only a cistern, we might soon exhaust His fullness. But who can drain a fountain?

A Christian man should so shine in his life that a person could not live with him a week without knowing the Gospel.

His mercy is so great that it forgives great sin to great sinners, after great lengths of time, and then gives great favors and great privileges, and raises us up to great enjoyments in the great heaven of the great God.

There is nothing little in God; His mercy is like Himself—it is infinite.

It may seem an easy thing to *wait*, but it is one of the postures which a Christian soldier learns not without years of teaching. Marching and quick marching are much easier to God's warriors than standing still.

The wreckers of Satan are always abroad, tempting the ungodly to sin under the name of pleasure.

Show the world that thy God is worth ten thousand worlds to thee.

The moment we glorify ourselves, since there is room for one glory only in the universe, we set ourselves up as rivals to the Most High.

May our hearts make Jesus their anchor, their rudder, their light-house, their life-boat, and their harbor.

A Christian ought to be a comforter, with kind words on his lips and sympathy in his heart; he should carry sunshine wherever he goes and diffuse happiness around him.

There are the common frames and feelings of repentance, and faith, and joy, and hope which are enjoyed by the entire family; but there is an upper realm of rapture, of communion, and conscious union with Christ which is far from being the common dwelling-place of believers.

The master-works of God are those men who stand in the midst of difficulties steadfast and unmovable.

It is scant love which the fire of persecution can dry up.

All that nature spins time will unravel, to the eternal confusion of all who are clothed therein.

If you would find the men who serve God the best, you must look for the men of the most faith.

Let your goodness be the only fault they can discover in you.

A great sin cannot destroy a Christian, but a little sin can make him miserable.

Sin is a loathsome and hateful thing, and no renewed heart can patiently endure it.

There is gold in the rocks which fringe the Pass of the Splugen, gold even in the stones which mend the roads, but there is too little of it to be worth extracting. Alas, how like too many books and sermons! Not so the Scriptures—they are much fine gold; their very dust is precious.

Get nearer to Jesus, and you will find yourself linked more and more in spirit to all who are, like yourself, supported by the same heavenly manna.

Our heavenly Father sends us frequent troubles *to try our faith*. If our faith be worth anything, it will stand the test. Gilt is afraid of fire, but gold is not; the *paste* gem dreads to be touched by the diamond, but the true jewel fears no test.

When God worketh without instruments doubtless He is glorified; but He hath Himself selected the plan of instrumentality as being that by which He is most magnified in the earth.

Why is it that some Christians, although they hear many sermons, make but slow advances in the divine life? Because they neglect their closets and do not thoughtfully meditate on God's Word.

Once let the truth of God obtain an entrance into the human heart and subdue the whole man unto itself, no power, human or infernal, can dislodge it.

When we are hard beset with this world, or with the severer trials within the Church, we find it a most blessed thing to pillow our head upon the bosom of our Saviour.

Our God has a method in providence by which he can succeed our endeavors beyond our expectation, or can defeat our plans to our confusion and dismay.

We will not forswear the sun till we find a better light, nor leave our Lord until a brighter lover shall appear; and, since this can never be, we will hold Him with a grasp immortal, and bind His name as a seal upon our arm.

Men trust good stewards with larger and larger sums, and so it frequently is with the Lord; He gives by cart-loads to those who give by bushels.

In a very wide sphere of observation I have noticed that the most generous Christians of my acquaintance have been always the most happy, and almost invariably the most prosperous.

Christ has paid the debt of His people to the last jot and tittle, and received the divine receipt; and unless God can be so unjust as to demand double payment for one debt, no soul for whom Jesus died as a substitute can ever be sent into hell.